E+**R**=O

E+R=O

~~The Most Important~~ Only Mindset for Success

KENT JULIAN

E+R=O
The Only Mindset for Success

Copyright © 2025 Kent Julian

All rights reserved. No portion of this book may be reproduced, stored in a retrieval system, or transmitted in any form or by any means—for example, electronic, mechanical, photocopy, recording, scanning, or other—except for brief questions in critical reviews or articles, without the prior written permission of the publisher.

Published by Live It Forward Publishing

ISBN: 978-0-9777363-8-6 paperback
ISBN: 978-0-9777363-5-5 hardcover
ISBN: 978-0-9777363-4-8 eBook

Book design by James Woosley, FreeAgentPress.com

Arrow image by Sergey Nivens @ 123RF.com

Subjects: Success, Personal Growth, Character, Resilience, Leadership, Motivation

For information about special discounts for bulk purchases, please contact Live It Forward LLC by emailing booking@kentjulian.com

For additional information about booking Kent Julian to speak, visit his website at www.KentJulian.com or email us at booking@kentjulian.com

Disclaimer: The opinions expressed in this book are for general information only and not intended to provide specific advice or recommendations for any individual. The author and publisher do not guarantee particular results by following the ideas, suggestions, or strategies written about in this book. The author and publisher shall have neither liability nor responsibility to anyone with respect to any loss or damage caused, or alleged to be caused, directly or indirectly by the information contained within this book.

VID: 20251124

To Jim Vaught, Stephen R. Covey,
and Jack Canfield.

Thank you for introducing me to E+R=O.

CONTENTS

INTRODUCTION: THE GIFT 1

PART 1: A PICTURE OF REALITY 12
   CHAPTER 1: MORE THAN A PAPERWEIGHT 15
   CHAPTER 2: THE WAY WE VIEW THINGS IS THE WAY WE DO THINGS 29

PART 2: THE FOUNDATION FOR SUCCESS 46
   CHAPTER 3: WHAT IS SUCCESS? 49
   CHAPTER 4: THE EXPANDING FENCE POSTS 61
   CHAPTER 5: IT'S A BIG UMBRELLA 75

PART 3: THE MUSCLE BEHIND GRIT 92
   CHAPTER 6: A WHOLE LOTTA ELVIS GOIN' ON 95
   CHAPTER 7: MUSCLE UP (WITHOUT STEROIDS) 115

CONCLUSION: TAKE A STEP 141

BONUS CHAPTER: E+R=O AND LEADERSHIP 156

AFTERWORD 179

ACKNOWLEDGMENTS 185

NOTES 187

RESOURCES 193

ABOUT THE AUTHOR 195

INTRODUCTION:
THE GIFT

"**W**HAT'S THE BEST GIFT I've ever given you?"

Have you ever asked a question that you knew beyond a shadow of a doubt what the answer would be?

When I asked my wife, Kathy, about the best gift I had ever given her, I already knew the answer. It consisted of five letters and started with the letter B.

For context, Kathy and I were high school students during what is arguably the best decade of music ever—the 1980s. However, our recollections of '80s music are drastically different.

I grew up in Atlanta, Georgia, and when I think of '80s music, the names that come to mind are Billy Joel, The Police, Pat Benatar, Phil Collins, and Bruce Springsteen's E Street Band. There are other great musicians from the 1980s, but these names pop into my head because I saw them in concert.

On the other hand, Kathy grew up in Peru, South America. Not only that, but she lived in Ayacucho—a small, rural town in the Andes Mountains. If you remember technology in the '80s, there was no internet or email. Mobile devices didn't exist either. Cable TV and computers? They were in their infancy, but neither had reached Ayacucho. Even landline telephones were all but non-existent, which meant Kathy's parents had to walk over a mile to access the closest phone.

So, Kathy is a young American teenager in the 1980s who loves American culture. However, since she's growing up in rural South America, she doesn't experience American culture in a timely manner. Instead, it arrives eight, nine, and even 10 years later. This means Kathy's favorite '80s music isn't '80s music at all. It's '70s music. And not just any '70s music, but mushy love songs from the '70s. For example, one of Kathy's favorite "1980s" bands is The Carpenters. Neil Diamond is one of her favorite solo artists. And have you heard of ABBA? If you're unfamiliar with these names, Google them. Each is a music icon from the 1970s.

Since I hinted that the gift I gave Kathy had five letters and started with the letter B, you may have guessed her all-time favorite "1980s" musician. He is a singer-songwriter best known for his love songs from the 1970s. He was so popular from 1974 to 1979 that he recorded five Top 10 albums. Yes, he is the one and only...

BARRY MANILOW.

(Too young to remember Barry Manilow? Google him and see if you agree that, while incredibly talented, he is one of the sappiest singers of all time.)

HAPPY BIRTHDAY!

Fast-forward a couple of decades. Kathy and I have been married for over 15 years, and she is about to celebrate a very important birthday. I won't tell you which one, but suffice to say, it started with the number four and ended with…let's just leave it there.

Additionally, you should know something about me. I'm not the world's greatest gift-giver. Not even close. Yet this was a milestone birthday, which meant I needed to step it up. That's why I spent weeks thinking about what to give her.

Then suddenly…

Out of nowhere…

An amazing, fantastic, wonderfully awful idea popped into my brain.

I could take Kathy to a…*gulp*…Barry Manilow concert.

You have to realize how agonizing this thought was for me. Even now, it pains me to type these words. To say that I am not a Barry Manilow fan is like saying I don't enjoy Brussels sprouts. I would never voluntarily listen to the first or eat the second. I can admit that Barry Manilow is talented. I can admit he's a great singer-songwriter. I can also admit Brussels sprouts are healthy, but that doesn't mean I eat them!

Yet the moment this Barry Manilow idea flashed across my mind, I couldn't think of another gift. Believe me, I tried. I prayed for a miracle. If I could imagine something else…anything else… that would make a better gift, I'd be off the hook. However, I finally realized that no matter how brutal the experience would be for me, it was the perfect gift for Kathy.

KATHY'S BEST GIFT

"What's the best gift I've ever given you?"

A few years after attending the concert, I asked Kathy this question, thinking I already knew the answer. But to my surprise, what I thought was the answer was only partially correct. Her answer did consist of five letters and started with the letter B, but it wasn't the Barry Manilow concert. It was Buzzy, our French Bulldog.[1]

Allow me to introduce Buzzy. As you can probably tell from his picture, Buzzy is neither charming nor obedient. My favorite description of him is that he's persnickety—sort of aloof and particular. He's not necessarily handsome either. Just look at him! He's so ugly, he's cute. It looks like his neck threw up or something.

Follow @BuzzyTheFrenchie on Instagram

But no matter what he looks like or how he acts, he is, by far, the best gift I've ever given Kathy. Growing up, she always wanted a dog as a pet. But in Ayacucho, dogs weren't considered pets. Most were strays that rummaged through garbage, and many were violent.

Once our three children were born, Kathy started talking about getting a dog. Truthfully, I wasn't too keen on the idea. I had grown up with dogs, and while I enjoyed them, I also knew how much care they required. Since our kiddos were young and our lives were full, I didn't think adding a puppy to the mix was a good idea. It took some time, but I eventually came around. Kathy and I started researching together and ultimately landed on a French Bulldog website. The moment we saw the pictures and read the descriptions, we knew we had found the perfect breed for our family.

A ONE-OF-A-KIND GIFT

Early in my career, I had the privilege of leading both small and large organizations. Now, as a professional speaker and business consultant, I'm honored to coach and train thousands of leaders each year. I'll share more later, but these experiences span a wide range—from coaching championship swim teams, to working directly with students and young professionals, to leading a division of a national association, to training frontline workers, educators, entrepreneurs, government leaders, business owners, and CEOs.

But my life didn't begin this way—not even close. I started out as an at-risk child with significant learning challenges. This meant academics were a constant struggle for me. Furthermore, when I finished high school, my SAT scores were so low that I had to enroll in a Development Studies program. I was required to pass all those courses before I could enroll in college—on probation. Needless to say, I was never in the running for the "Most Likely to Succeed" award.

So, what changed? How did I go from "least likely to succeed" to experiencing success in several rewarding careers? And how have I been fortunate enough to enjoy so many other blessings, such as a healthy marriage, a strong family, excellent relationships, two thriving businesses, meaningful community impact, and more?

It's because I was given a gift during one of the darker moments of my life. It was a one-of-a-kind gift that has positively shaped me from the inside out. Things didn't change immediately. In fact, it took 20 years before I could clearly articulate and explain the gift. But make no mistake, it transformed me. It transformed how I see life. It transformed how I think about life. It even transformed how I respond to life. Indeed, the more I implement this gift, the more capable and confident I become at handling whatever life throws at me.

I wrote this book because I want to do for you what others did for me. I want to pass this gift along to you. Even more, I want to do so in a way that allows you to understand its brilliance and value more quickly than I did. (I doubt you'll need 20 years to read this book.)

But before we dive in, let's take a moment to explore a few big-picture ideas that will help you navigate the life-changing, inside-out journey ahead.

WHAT THIS GIFT IS NOT

Let's start with what this gift is not.

It Is Not a BIG Gift. We're often tempted to believe that the best gifts are the big ones. But as the old saying goes, sometimes the best gifts come in small packages. This is especially true when it comes to personal growth and professional development. It's easy to assume that big results require big steps or dramatic changes—like taking Kathy to the Barry Manilow concert. But more often, success is built on taking small, meaningful actions—like the Buzzy gift. When these small steps are taken consistently, they lead to the big successes we hope to achieve. And here's the thing: nothing empowers you to take those small, meaningful steps more than this gift.

It Is Not a NEW Gift. What I mean by this statement is that this gift doesn't come from outside of us. It's a choice we're all capable of making. Therefore, to access it, all you have to do is recognize what the gift is and learn how to draw it out.

It Is Not ORIGINAL with Me. On the dedication page, I shared the names of the three individuals most responsible for giving me this gift. Since then, I have devoted much of my career to researching, writing, and speaking about it. Over the years, I discovered that this gift has been around for quite a while. As this book will show, it is one of the most thoroughly researched theories in the field of personal development. And while it goes by many different names, the fundamental concept remains the same, regardless of the terminology used.

WHAT THIS GIFT IS

So, what exactly is this gift?

It's not a physical gift. As just mentioned, it comes from the world of personal development. We'll dive into the details shortly, but for now, here's a quick snapshot.

It Is a Picture of REALITY. In other words, it's how the real world works best. Therefore, if you want to be successful (and we'll define success in Chapter Three), this gift gives you the best chance.

It Is the Foundation for SUCCESS. Speaking of success, one reason this gift is so valuable is that it serves as an umbrella under which all success principles fall. Or, to put it another way, it's how you get success principles working for you instead of against you.

It Is the Muscle Behind GRIT. Determination and commitment are essential for success, but even the most resilient individuals can falter and throw in the towel when things get tough. Yet this gift gives you the grit needed to push through those challenging moments. It is why some people, who are not necessarily loaded with natural talent, end up outperforming those who are more gifted than they are. It is also why certain individuals persevere when almost everyone else gives up.

MY PROMISE TO YOU

Earlier, when I shared about my career and personal life, it might have sounded like I think I have it all together. I don't. Like you, I am a fellow traveler trying to navigate life. Sometimes I struggle. Other times, I succeed. Most often, I'm doing a bit of both. So, while this book is about experiencing success, I am not writing as someone who has arrived. Again, like you, I'm moving forward step by step, striving to learn, grow, and get better along the way.

However, I am writing as someone who has extensive first-hand experience with the difference this gift can make. For one, as already mentioned, it helped me overcome my at-risk behavior and gave me the confidence to tackle the learning challenges I faced (and still face today). Two, it has made my decision-making clearer, which has, in turn, made life easier to navigate. Three, it has also instilled a strength of character that goes far beyond anything I inherited from my DNA. It's safe to say that most people want to experience these kinds of benefits for themselves.

Yet beyond what this gift has done for me, I've had the privilege of seeing it positively impact hundreds, if not thousands, of people in the businesses, organizations, and associations I speak to each year. Many, *amazingly* so! I'll introduce you to a few of these individuals in the upcoming pages, but let me be clear from the start: there is nothing particularly special about these people. No royal pedigrees or superhuman talents. Just like me, they are ordinary people who discovered an extraordinary gift that has dramatically enhanced their lives from the inside out. And I promise, it can do the same for you.

Finally, it must be evident by now that I believe the personal development gift you are about to receive will help you like no other. However, I also realize that once you've read this book, having to comb back through these pages each time you want to remember something is not the best use of your time. That's why I created a collection of resources to use as a quick reference point for applying this gift. Consider them a bonus for having read the book. They're all available now at **KENTJULIAN.COM/ RESPONSEBOOK** or by using the QR code below.

★ ★ ★ ★ ★

Now, let's unwrap this gift together. As we do, I believe you'll discover that you already know something about it, because, as mentioned, it is a choice you are capable of making. At the same time, you'll uncover a depth and richness that go beyond your imagination. That's because this is a gift that keeps on giving, and with each layer, it transforms you—from the inside out—for the better.

Part 1
A PICTURE OF REALITY

CHAPTER 1:

MORE THAN A PAPERWEIGHT

MOST HUMAN-INTEREST STORIES DO not receive front-page coverage. The one you are about to read is no exception, but it should have been. Steve Meyer was an X-ray technician who lived in Georgia. Yet this story isn't about his work. It's about his hobby. He was a rock collector.

Personally, I've never been drawn to rock collecting. I'm not someone who enjoys wandering through mountains or forests in search of them, and I've often wondered what people do with the rocks they find. Do they keep them in a garden? Or display them on a shelf at home? For me, being "outdoorsy" usually means riding my bike on the local greenway, and Earth Science wasn't exactly my strongest subject. So, rock collecting has never really been in my wheelhouse.

Steve Meyer, on the other hand, loved hiking the Appalachian Mountains and collecting rocks. During one weekend trek to North Carolina, he and a friend found a rock he especially liked. Upon returning home, instead of doing whatever he did with the rest of his collection, he took this rock to his office to use as a paperweight. In case you are unclear about its purpose, a paperweight is a heavy object (like a rock) that is placed on top of a stack of papers to prevent them from blowing around the room when the ceiling fan is on or the windows are open.

So, Steve Meyer used his favorite new rock as a paperweight. Isn't this a great human-interest story so far?

Well, a few months later, a gentleman visited Steve's office. When he saw the rock, his eyes grew to the size of Wham-O Frisbees as his jaw dropped to the floor.

"What is that?!" he shouted.

Steve Meyer mumbled, "Ummmm... a rock."

"That's no rock—that's a sapphire!"

This individual was an expert gem cutter. After examining the sapphire, he told Steve, "You better get a safety deposit box because, by its mere size, it's worth $150,000." A few months later, Steve took the sapphire to another gem cutter in Texas. This gentleman informed him that the jewel could likely be sold for more than the Star of America, which was a sapphire that had recently received a $4 million purchase offer.

$4 MILLION!

And Steve Meyer was using it as a paperweight.[1]

MY INTRODUCTION TO E+R=O

The title of this book is *E+R=O*, so you have probably guessed that the gift I hinted at in the Introduction has something to do with this equation. Before defining E+R=O, let me share how I was introduced to it. Interestingly, I became acquainted with this mindset long before I heard the equation. In fact, the equation wasn't even part of the vocabulary of the person who introduced me to this way of thinking.

In elementary school, I was a loser and knew it. It's not as though I was depressed or unhappy; I was a friendly kid who got along with almost everyone. However, I did struggle. Academically, I had a significant speech impediment and could not pronounce the sounds associated with the letters "f, g, j, k, l, r, s, v, z, ch, sh, th, and related consonant blends."[2] Additionally, by the time I reached third grade, my teacher had a meeting with my parents and asked how I had passed the previous grades without being able to read. Simply put, I wasn't the sharpest tack in the box.

Physically, I wasn't much to look at either. I was short, chubby, had thick brown-framed glasses, and wore Toughskin Jeans. If you aren't familiar with Toughskins, envision the dorkiest pair of pants a kid could wear. No joke, they actually had knee pads built into the fabric. Not exactly a confidence booster for a self-conscious little boy.

However, what was most difficult for me was my lack of athletic ability. I loved sports, but my arms and legs didn't support that passion. Let's just say when it came time to choose kickball teams, I prayed not to be picked last. At least that way, I knew I wasn't the biggest loser on the playground.

When I started middle school, I hit a growth spurt. I shot up so fast that by the beginning of eighth grade, I was almost as tall as I am now. Along with this growth came some athletic ability—not a ton, but enough that I decided to try out for the middle school basketball team in seventh grade.

Jim Vaught, the middle school coach, decided to keep 15 players that year. When he met with me, he told me I was the last person selected for the team. The conversation was not an "Aren't-You-Lucky" speech, but more of an "I-Believe-in-You" chat. He told me I probably wouldn't see a ton of playing time, but next year could be a different story if I worked hard during the season. To be honest, I wasn't really listening. I was just thrilled to make the team. In my mind, I would never be a real athlete, so even being associated with athletes was a step up from my perennial loser status. I still wasn't confident, but at least now, I could fake like I was.

During the season, I made a major personal mistake—something I am still ashamed of to this day. The details aren't necessary; just know it was *major*. When Mr. Vaught called me into his office to confront me about my transgression, I had no idea I had been caught. When he dropped the bomb, I was devastated. The wrongdoing was bad enough. But in that moment, I realized my parents, teachers, and a basketball coach who believed in me were all disappointed. All the confidence that had been budding within me was cut short.

Or was it?

Mr. Vaught helped turn a potentially devastating situation into a positive watershed moment in my life. He was firm. He was tough. And he was visibly disappointed. Yet he still believed in me. I could sense it. I saw it in his eyes and heard it in his words.

Even in the midst of confronting me with tough truths and saying things that were difficult to hear, I knew he believed I was a special kid with a special future. He clearly communicated that my tomorrow did not need to be created from my yesterday and that my future was still in the future. He challenged me to own up to my wrongdoing, seek forgiveness, learn from it, and move on.

At the end of the season, Mr. Vaught pulled me aside for another chat. The incident happened only a few weeks earlier, so I had been avoiding Coach. I saw him in math class and at basketball practice, but I always kept my distance. So at first, when he wanted to talk, I was afraid he would rehash my transgression. Instead, all he said was, "Kent, I think you could get significant playing time next year if you work hard this summer. I really do!" When the next year rolled around, not only was I starting, but I also led the team in scoring.

At the awards ceremony, Mr. Vaught stood in front of a packed gym and said something along these lines, "I want to recognize Kent Julian. Last season, he was the last person picked for the team. This summer, he dedicated himself to practicing four to five hours a day. Because of his efforts, he is our most improved player, our leading scorer, and our most valuable player."

Nice words, huh? Decades later, I have a hard time writing them without getting choked up. But honestly, Jim Vaught left out one crucial detail. I accomplished those things *because* he believed in me. If he had handled my watershed moment any differently, those words would have never been uttered—at least not about me. My relationship with Mr. Vaught—a teacher and coach who saw me at my very worst, yet chose to believe in my absolute best—was what inspired me.

Because he believed in me, I started to believe.

And this belief didn't only affect my basketball skills. Confidence started to spill over into other areas of my life as well.

And that brings us back to the equation.

WHAT IS E+R=O?

So, what is E+R=O?

E+R=O is a mindset that stands for *Event + RESPONSE = Outcome*.

Yet here's the problem. No one comes out of the womb embracing an E+R=O mindset. Instead, almost by default, we instinctively believe E=O, which stands for *Event = Outcome*.

I'm not sure why we have a natural bent toward an E=O mindset. Perhaps our internal wiring is messed up, and E=O is automatically embedded in our DNA.[3] Or maybe it's because we're lazy and there's one less letter to remember. Whatever the reason, humans are inclined to believe that the events (*E*) they face determine the outcomes (*O*) they experience. This is why so many people develop victim mentalities. If events determine outcomes, then there isn't much we can do to shape our lives. Since most events are beyond our control, we're just recipients of whatever happens to us. We benefit when events are good, but we become victims when events are bad.[4]

However…

If you choose to add an R to the equation, everything changes!

Those who embrace an E+R=O mindset (*Event + RESPONSE = Outcome*) understand that most events, whether good or bad, are beyond their control. Yet they also realize that they can *choose* their response. And by conscientiously choosing their response, they shape the outcomes they experience. Or, explained differently, they move the leverage for determining outcomes away from the events they face and place it onto the choices they make. This means they can take a negative event and turn it into a positive outcome. They can even face adversity and turn it into an advantage. I call people who adopt an E+R=O mindset *Response-ABLE* because they are *able* to choose how they respond, regardless of the circumstances they face.

To sum it up, life always gives us feedback, and E=O or E+R=O are the two mindsets through which we filter that feedback. Since whatever we focus on expands in our minds, either the E (*event*) that happens to us expands or the R (*response*) we choose expands. For instance, if we focus on the E, the circumstances of that event will grow and gain more influence over us. However, if we instead focus on our R, our ability to respond will expand, giving us more options for shaping the O (*outcome*) we experience. This means every event, whether good or bad, can serve as a learning experience that helps us grow and get better. We get to choose, and that choice is a gift!

In light of this explanation, the purpose of this book is to equip you to proactively choose, on a daily basis, an E+R=O mindset instead of passively surrendering to an E=O mindset. This is crucial because E+R=O is the only mindset for success.

LEARNED HELPLESSNESS VS. LEARNED OPTIMISM

To better understand the E=O versus E+R=O mindsets, let's examine studies on *learned helplessness* versus *learned optimism*.

As a graduate student at the University of Pennsylvania in the 1960s, Martin Seligman researched the causes and conditions of mental illness. He and his colleagues discovered that hardships and setbacks alone don't necessarily lead to helplessness. Instead, helplessness is often a learned behavior shaped more by how a person *perceives* negative events rather than by the events themselves. That is to say, when people view hardships deterministically and believe they can do nothing about them, this perspective leads to a phenomenon Seligman calls "learned helplessness." And what exactly is learned helplessness? It's "the quitting response that follows from the belief that whatever you do doesn't matter."[5]

As a side note, the longer Seligman and his colleagues conducted their research, the more they realized the devastating effects of the pessimism caused by learned helplessness. It leads to symptoms such as "anxiety, inertia, worry, depression, poor physical health, and failure even when success is attainable."[6]

Interestingly, after more than a decade of research, Seligman moved in a new direction. Instead of continuing his exploration of learned helplessness, he shifted his attention to combating the problem. This led him to develop a new field of study, which he called "learned optimism," and eventually resulted in a book by the same name. Without getting into the weeds, here are the fundamental findings of his research:

- Optimists and pessimists both encounter bad events.
- Where they differ is in their "Explanatory Style."
- Pessimists see "permanent" and "pervasive" causes for bad events.

- Optimists assume bad events are "temporary" and "specific."[7]

In other words, pessimists not only believe that bad events will persist, but they also allow bad events to bleed over into other areas of their lives. By contrast, optimists do not believe bad events will continue indefinitely, and they seek to compartmentalize the impact of a bad event to the specific area of life it is affecting.

These studies provide fabulous insight into the difference between an E=O and E+R=O mindset. Two people can experience the same adverse event, yet each can interpret it quite differently. And it is the *interpretation* of the event rather than the event itself that usually leads to the outcome experienced. Put simply, perspective changes everything.

For instance, let's use the example of a job loss as a negative event. Since people with an E=O mindset are prone to develop learned helplessness, they will assume permanent and pervasive causes are to blame. This means they are likely to choose one or more of the following reactions:

- Self-pity
- Criticism
- Defensiveness
- Blaming others
- Resentment and holding grudges
- Inability to see other options or opportunities

On the other hand, people who adopt an E+R=O mindset will likely develop learned optimism and interpret the loss of their job differently. This is not to say they won't feel upset or hurt; they will experience disappointment like anyone else. However, unlike an E=O person, their focus will not be limited solely to the event. They will also consider their response. And the more they hone in on their response, the more they will interpret the job loss as temporary and due to specific causes.

Therefore, rather than feeling helpless or getting stuck in the blame game, the E+R=O person will move forward with hope. They will let go of what they cannot control (i.e., *event*) and take ownership of what they can control (i.e., *response*). This opens their eyes to better options and new opportunities. In the job loss scenario, they will say things like:

- "I messed up, but I can learn from this experience and improve."
- "I was treated unfairly, but now I know how to avoid that situation in the future."
- "I wish this didn't happen, but I have more clarity about what to do next."

To be clear, an E+R=O mindset does not mean you turn a blind eye to the event and pretend it didn't happen. We have all met people who are so overly optimistic that they ignore reality. However, that is not an E+R=O mindset. It is E=O in disguise. It is a person pretending to choose their response when they are actually refusing to deal with what is happening.

By contrast, E+R=O means that you acknowledge the event, no matter how undesirable, undeserving, unfair, or unpleasant it may be. It also means that, moving forward, you determine how your actions and attitude can shape the outcome you experience. Granted, this approach sounds tough because, in many cases, it is. However, it is also the far more beneficial path to follow. Otherwise, you give control of your life over to the very thing which you have no control over—the event. Alternatively, when you consciously choose your response, you create options for yourself. Even more, the difficulties you encounter also become learning experiences, which means you can grow wiser, stronger, and gain more confidence along the way. Eventually, you realize you can face any roadblock, obstacle, or adversity life throws at you.

This, my friend, is precisely how E+R=O works! It helps you develop learned optimism instead of falling prey to learned helplessness. It equips you to interpret events as temporary and specific rather than permanent and pervasive.

#1 SUCCESS PRINCIPLE

This book is dedicated to the three people who helped me discover E+R=O. The first was Jim Vaught, the middle school basketball coach I wrote about earlier. While he never used the equation E+R=O or the term Response-ABLE, he introduced me to the concept.

Then, early in my career, I read Stephen Covey's groundbreaking book *The 7 Habits of Highly Effective People*. The first habit, "Be Proactive," thoroughly explores the idea of personal responsibility. He even points out that the word "responsibility" means "the ability to choose your response."[8] This book is one of my all-time favorites and was incredibly influential to me as a young professional; it played a crucial role in deepening the roots of what I had learned from Jim Vaught.

A few years later, I attended a training event where Jack Canfield briefly spoke about E+R=O during his presentation. He had learned the equation from Dr. Robert Resnick, and this simple concept encapsulated nearly everything I had learned from Jim Vaught and Stephen Covey. But even more, it served as a catalyst for systematizing how I would think about these things moving forward.

I will never forget the day I sat in Mr. Vaught's office as a middle schooler being confronted about my wrongdoing. Similarly, I will never forget the day I heard Jack Canfield explain the E+R=O equation. These two incidents were separated by approximately 20 years. The first was a crisis moment I created. The second was a personal development moment I pursued. And although the experiences were as different as night and day, they served as the bookends of my introduction to E+R=O. The first initiated my journey away from victimhood toward being Response-ABLE. The second was the culmination of all I had learned during those 20 years and served as a launching pad for how I wanted to live moving forward.

As soon as Canfield published his best-selling book, *The Success Principles*, I picked up a copy. In it, he shares 64 success principles, but it's clear from the start that the very first principle is the most important. In Chapter One, he writes, "If you want to be successful, you have to take 100 percent responsibility for everything that you experience in your life. This includes the level of your achievements, the results you produce, the quality of your relationships, the state of your health and physical fitness, your income, your debts, your feelings—everything!"[9] He also says, "The real truth—and the one lesson this whole book is based on—is that there is only one person responsible for the quality of the life you live. That person is *you*."[10]

Did you get that?

Jack Canfield, a pioneer in the fields of personal development and peak performance, states that if you do not take 100 percent responsibility for your life, none of the other success principles in his book will help. To be more blunt, he is saying if you do not become Response-ABLE, you can throw the other 63 principles in the trash. They will not work for you. This means, according to Canfield, E+R=O is the mindset that gets all the success principles working for you instead of against you.

THE 4 MILLION DOLLAR PAPERWEIGHT

We began this chapter with Steve Meyer and his sapphire. Unbeknownst to him, he was using a $4 million jewel as a paperweight. What a picture of how we—myself included—mistakenly overlook or underutilize the gift of E+R=O.

First, just as Steve already had the sapphire in his possession, each of us has access to the E+R=O mindset. It's already in our possession, whether we realize it or not.

Second, deep down, most people know that to experience success, they must take personal responsibility for their lives. Having this type of mindset is what empowers us to own our lives instead of allowing life to own us.

Yet third, while E+R=O is an invaluable gift already in our possession, it often sits in our lives like a paperweight. As we have discussed, humans are naturally inclined to believe E=O. They assume good outcomes only come from good events, and that bad events inevitably lead to bad outcomes. Even though this is flawed thinking, it is what we believe by default. Of course, we can combat this wrong-headed thinking by developing an E+R=O mindset, but most people don't do that. Instead, they overlook or ignore E+R=O. As a result, it ends up just lying around in their life like a forgotten, worthless paperweight.

★ ★ ★ ★ ★

> There you have it—E+R=O is a hidden gem with the power to dramatically change your life, and it's already in your possession. Now that we have uncovered its potential, the question becomes: How do you apply it in your life?
>
> Let's start by examining the lenses through which we view the world because, as you will soon see, the way we view things is the way we do things.

CHAPTER 2:

THE WAY WE VIEW THINGS IS THE WAY WE DO THINGS

HERE'S A STORY I came across years ago. See if it captures your attention as much as it did mine.

> *Several years ago, scientists conducted an interesting experiment. They strapped a strange set of eyeglasses, which looked like binoculars, on several people. The participants willingly wore these glasses every hour they were awake. Inside the lenses, several mirrors enabled the wearers to see everything upside down. At first, they tripped over furniture*

and were unable to walk. They could barely sit upright without falling over.

After a few weeks of wearing the glasses, their eyes adjusted, and they were able to see everything right side up again. Not only could they sit up and walk without difficulty, but they were also able to drive through traffic and ride a bicycle without any problems. The human brain made adjustments, and each person was no longer aware of seeing upside down. As far as they were concerned, they were seeing right side up.

Little did they know, however, that when the glasses were removed, the experiment had just begun. One by one, as the participants removed the glasses, they immediately fell over. Their brains had adjusted so well to seeing through the inverted glasses that when the participants removed them, everything they saw seemed to be upside down. It took several weeks for their brains to readjust to not wearing the glasses, but eventually, each of the participants was able to see the world right side up again.[1]

A PICTURE OF REALITY

The story above is more than an illustration—it's a mirror. It reflects how our perspective shapes the way we respond to the world around us. For example, E+R=O (*Event + RESPONSE = Outcome*) clarifies how the real world works…or at least, how it works best. How does it do this? By giving us right-side-up lenses. Rather than accepting the upside-down premise that events alone determine outcomes, E+R=O shows that our responses also play a role in our outcomes, often more so than the events themselves.

Most people, however, lack this kind of right-side-up clarity. Operating from an E=O mindset (*Event = Outcome*), they believe outcomes are determined solely by external events. This means circumstances are 100 percent culpable for every outcome in a person's life. Such thinking is dangerous because it leads to what we discussed earlier—learned helplessness. And if left unchecked, learned helplessness can easily turn into something much worse—a *victim mentality*.

Similar to learned helplessness, a victim mentality believes that when bad things happen, there is nothing a person can do to change the situation. However, it goes a step further. Instead of just feeling helpless, individuals with a victim mentality get exacerbated and start acting out. They blame circumstances and people for their problems. They lash out in anger when challenged. They even lack empathy for others who struggle, because in their minds, this robs them of the recognition they deserve for their problems.

In the real world, however, people with a victim mentality rarely gain the notoriety they seek. They typically become joyless individuals who no one wants to be around. They have a knack for seeing problems rather than solutions. And they refuse to take responsibility for anything, which means nothing is ever their fault.

Again, this is upside-down thinking. It's also not how the real world works (or at least not how it works best). While this approach might bring short-term gratification, no one can truly move forward in life until they take responsibility for improving their situation.

To prove this point, consider the heroes you have admired over the years (I'll share a few of mine in Chapter Seven). You can probably assemble a list of five or 10 people pretty quickly. Some you know personally. Others you have read about or heard their stories. They likely come from different backgrounds and upbringings. Each has different skills and abilities, and each has faced unique struggles. But I bet they all share one thing in common...

They live E+R=O instead of E=O.

That's because heroes, whether famous or not, refuse to play the role of a victim. No matter who wrongs them or how badly they are taken advantage of, they still take ownership of their lives. They are Response-ABLE, which is precisely why we look up to them. They are the ones who say, "No matter how hard it is or how long it takes, I *will* live it forward and overcome the obstacles I face."

TAKING A CLOSER LOOK

Before moving on, it's crucial we clarify something. There is a fundamental difference between being a victim of an event and having a victim mentality. The first is something real. The second is an upside-down belief based on a flawed perspective. Since we just addressed the falsehoods of a victim mentality, let's take a closer look at the fact that bad things happen to people, and not all events are created equal. Some events are more devastating than others. For instance, it's one thing to be overlooked for a job promotion; it's quite another to experience physical abuse or be diagnosed with a chronic illness.

Let me assure you that when I suggest adding an R to an E=O life, I do not take events lightly—especially those that are harmful or destructive. As you know from my personal story, I encountered some rough terrain at the outset of my life. I wasn't a smart kid. I wasn't even average. And while I faced obstacles early on, I also recognize that the start of my story was significantly less severe than the start of many other people's stories. Sure, I had to overcome learning challenges, but I know others who have faced greater hardships. Serious illnesses. Neglect. Racism. Abuse. Abandonment. Overwhelming poverty. The death of a parent in childhood.

Yet the fact is, my story is my story.

And guess what?

Your story is your story.

You have to live your story.

And I have to live my story.

Your story might be easier than mine. Or it might be ten times more difficult. That's not the point. The point is we each have a story, and each of us must live out our *own* story. As a matter of fact, there are three truths about each of our stories:

- Our story is our story and nobody else's.
- We cannot change what has been written in our story—that ink has already dried.
- We can, however, take 100 percent responsibility for what is left to be written—that ink is still in our pens.

These three truths are why focusing on your Rs instead of your Es is so essential. This statement is not intended to trivialize challenging or hurtful events. It is merely to point out reality. And while it might sound harsh, the truth is reality can be harsh. It's tough to realize you cannot change past events. It's also tough to know you cannot dictate future events. The only thing you have 100 percent control over is your response. Therefore, going forward, the best thing you can do is take ownership of how you respond to present and future events. When you do, you take ownership of your life. You move away from only allowing events to happen *to* you and toward tailoring the events you experience, even the bad ones, to happen *for* you. This does not mean difficult events become easier or less painful. It simply means your responses will have a greater influence on shaping your outcomes.

So yes, this is a tough reality. But it's also the truth. And sharing the truth candidly and directly, even if it's tough, is the most benevolent approach in communication. It helps us see reality right side up as it truly is, instead of distorting it into something it's not.

WHAT ABOUT GOOD EVENTS?

One more pertinent thought about events must be considered before circling back to how E+R=O works in the real world. You have probably noticed that the examples of Es described so far have been negative events. I've used words like obstacles, challenges, adversities, and roadblocks. What's interesting, however, is that even when we experience positive events, our lives will still shrink if we have an E=O mindset.

For instance, as a former swim coach, I worked with thousands of young swimmers. One of the most gifted swimmers I ever coached was a young lady who, early on, stood head and shoulders above her peers (*event*). Since she was dripping with talent, she didn't appreciate the importance of developing character traits such as discipline, commitment, and a strong work ethic. Why work hard when you win every race by half the length of the pool?

I coached another young swimmer who was blessed with some natural ability, but not nearly as much as the first swimmer (*event*). This second swimmer, however, developed the character traits that the first swimmer ignored (*response*).

Because the first swimmer had more natural talent than the second, she dominated her events for years. Throughout elementary and middle school, she was always the high-point winner in her age group. However, things changed when these athletes reached their sophomore year of high school. Swimmer number two started winning races while swimmer number one struggled to compete. By the end of high school, the fortunes of these two swimmers had flipped. Although the second swimmer never won a first-place ribbon until she was 14, she ultimately earned a scholarship to a nationally ranked university. The other swimmer, who had won hundreds—perhaps even a thousand—first-place ribbons before age 14, saw her swimming career become a story of missed opportunities.

If this swimming analogy doesn't resonate with you, here's another example of how a good event can cause your life to shrink if you have an E=O mindset. I know of two individuals who received similar inheritances. One used his to start a business, eventually making him a millionaire. The other purchased a brand-new automobile with all the bells and whistles, plus a five-star vacation package. Today, the person who started the business has the resources to enjoy nice cars, vacations, and many other activities. Additionally, his investments continue to grow, and he makes numerous charitable donations. The other individual has nothing left. The car is gone, and the vacation is a distant memory. But that's not the worst of it. Because he missed opportunities to learn, grow, and develop, his life is smaller than it would be if he had only made different decisions.

In his outstanding book *David and Goliath*, Malcolm Gladwell explains how positive events are not always beneficial. In fact, they can be downright detrimental. Early on, Gladwell lays out the book's purpose by writing, "[This] is a book about what happens when ordinary people confront giants. By 'giants,' I mean powerful opponents of all kinds—from armies and mighty warriors to disability, misfortune, and oppression."[2] He goes on to point out that his research demonstrates that "what we consider valuable in our world often arises out of…lopsided conflicts [*event*], because the act of facing overwhelming odds [*response*] produces greatness and beauty [*outcome*]."[3]

What a compelling picture of how an E+R=O mindset can turn tough events into positive outcomes. But Gladwell's words also demonstrate that the opposite is true—too much ease and comfort can hinder a person with an E=O mindset. For example, when someone faces overwhelming odds, it can inspire greatness in that person, provided they are determined to overcome the adversity. By contrast, when events are too easy, people often become complacent and fail to develop the mental fortitude and grit necessary for success. So, while none of us wants to face difficult events, something inherent in them causes us to grow wiser, stronger, and more confident as we learn to overcome them. To use additional words from Gladwell about the purpose of his book, "Each chapter tells the story of a different person—famous or unknown, ordinary or brilliant—who has faced an outsized challenge and been *forced to respond*" (emphasis added).⁴

The bottom line to the swimming and inheritance examples, as well as Gladwell's book, is this: No matter what events you encounter, living E=O never ends well. Whether facing difficulty, overcoming giants, enjoying comfort, or experiencing blessings, E=O always creates an upside-down perspective that shrinks your life.

THE REST OF THE STORY

The gift of E+R=O literally changed my life. I know this sounds like hyperbole, but it's not. And although I feel uncomfortable writing about personal experiences, I do so in this book. The discomfort stems from not wanting to shine a spotlight on myself. As I have already stated, I'm an ordinary guy. Nothing special. Nothing spectacular. Anything extraordinary in my life has come about largely because of E+R=O. All I've done is apply what I've learned (and, as you will discover, not always that well). Therefore, the positive personal stories I share are more about what happens when you apply this gift than they are about any special talent or ability I possess.

With this in mind, I would like to provide some additional context about my middle school years. These details will shed more light on the power of E+R=O.

As an at-risk kid with a speech impediment and learning challenge, I felt dumb from the moment I started kindergarten.

37

Not only did I feel stupid, but I believed I *was* stupid. While this belief negatively impacted me academically, it also shattered my self-confidence in other areas, such as social situations, personal self-worth, and even leisure activities. As stated, my favorite recreational endeavors revolved around sports, but since my arms and legs didn't support that passion, it was merely one more way I felt inadequate.

The first time I recall feeling a glimmer of hope that I wasn't a complete loser was when my middle school basketball coach introduced me to the essence of E+R=O.[5] Here was Mr. Vaught—a role model I looked up to—who believed I could be better than I thought I could be. He went out of his way to show me how to improve as a basketball player. He even set up a summer program for me to follow. He promised, "If you do these drills for 30 minutes a day, three times a week, you will improve."

No one had ever done anything like this for me before. Up until that point, every coach I played for didn't want me on their team. None of them ever said that aloud, but it was painfully clear they thought it. Furthermore, I agreed with them. My athletic ability was so nonexistent that even I realized they had to find ways to put me in the game without jeopardizing their chances of winning. Their jobs would have been much easier if I hadn't been on the team.

Jim Vaught, on the other hand, saw something in me even though he picked me last for the team. And he didn't just see something; he went out of his way to communicate what he saw. Then, unbelievably, he took a personal interest in helping me see that vision too. This was incredible on its own, but looking back, I still can't believe he did all that while having to confront my

The Way We View Things Is the Way We Do Things

wrongdoing. You see, Mr. Vaught wasn't only a basketball coach and math teacher. He was also an assistant principal. That meant he had to deal with the turmoil I created. Nevertheless, in the midst of this mess (and all my guilt and shame), he encouraged me to get better. For some reason, instead of seeing an at-risk kid, he saw an at-potential kid. I'm not sure why, but I am forever grateful.

How did I respond? For the first time in my life, I took ownership of something. Coach Vaught said if I wanted to improve, I should do specific drills for 30 minutes a day, three times a week. But let's be clear, the other guys on the team were far more athletic than I was. This meant I had to work four or five times harder to get any playing time. That's why I threw Coach Vaught's "30 minutes a day, three times a week" suggestion into the trash can. It had to be two, three, and even four hours a day for me. I also rode my crimson-red, 10-speed Schwinn bike to the local gym on Mondays, Wednesdays, and Fridays. On those days, from 11:30 AM to 1:30 PM, I played pickup games against grown men during their lunch break.

Jump ahead six months...

I knew I had gotten better, but I couldn't gauge by how much. Truthfully, I was just hoping to be good enough not to sit the bench for entire games. Once preseason practice started, however, it didn't take long to realize how much better I had become. Most guys were still more athletic than I was, but my basketball skills had become more honed than theirs. By the end of the first few days of practice, I was the go-to player on the team. And by the end of the season, I had outscored the next closest player by double. This transformation from the last person chosen to being the go-to player is why Jim Vaught named me Most Improved Player, Most Valuable Player, and High Scorer at the awards ceremony.

However, to ensure we keep the spotlight on the gift Mr. Vaught gave me rather than on my basketball skills, here's a less flattering fact. I went on to play high school basketball, but I never had another season like that eighth-grade season—not even close. For example, I scored 100 points during that eighth-grade season. If you add up all four of my high school seasons, I don't think I scored a total of 100 points combined.

As you can see, this story has little to do with my basketball skills. Instead, it's about my first encounter with taking ownership of my attitude and actions. The stage was a basketball court, but the drama that unfolded was realizing that my responses could significantly impact my outcomes. This was my first lesson in understanding the difference between E=O and E+R=O.

DIFFERENT LENSES. DIFFERENT REALITIES.

"The Way We View Things Is the Way We Do Things."[6] We have explored several key realities about life, and the title of this chapter highlights how the lenses of E=O versus E+R=O cause us to view (and do) things very differently.

First, we don't control the vast majority of events that happen to us. We do not control the weather, the economy, the biases of other people, the actions taken by others, or even random events that occur. Most people, whether they are wearing E=O or E+R=O lenses, realize this is true.

A second key reality is that people who wear E=O lenses view life from an upside-down perspective. In their minds, the only component that influences their outcomes is the events that happen to them. This mindset leads to learned helplessness and eventually a victim mentality. E+R=O lenses, on the other hand, help individuals realize they don't have to become victims of events. Although some events may be unpleasant, undesirable, or unfair, everyone can be responsible for their choices. Having this kind of right-side-up vision enables people to shift power away from what they cannot control—*events*—and grant more influence to the one thing they do control—their *response*.

A third important reality is that good events don't automatically translate into good outcomes. If you view life through the upside-down lenses of E=O, your life will still shrink regardless of whether events are good or bad. That's because, instead of investing *in* your responses, you will passively rely *on* events to shape your outcomes.

As you can see, the way we view things dramatically influences the way we do things. In other words, *how* we view life impacts *what* attitudes and actions we adopt. Viewing things through the upside-down lenses of E=O causes us to believe that events determine outcomes. Alternatively, E+R=O lenses create right-side-up clarity. Yes, events play a role in our outcomes, but how we choose to respond plays a much more significant role.

A REALISTIC VIEW OF E+R=O AND YOUR LIFE

Finally, as we transition to the second part of this book and focus on the role E+R=O plays in success, I'd like to tie up a few loose ends. While these ideas are somewhat random, they are nevertheless crucial because each helps us move forward with a realistic view of E+R=O and the realities of life.

Let's start with something I mentioned earlier—that E+R=O brings clarity to how the real world works (or at least how it works best). Does this sound like I'm speaking out of both sides of my mouth? Seriously, which is it? Is E+R=O how the real world works? Or, is it how the real world works best?

The answer to both is yes.

Perhaps you've heard the phrase "you reap what you sow." It's a common idiom in wisdom literature and many religious beliefs. It means that the actions you take determine the results you get.

While this saying often reflects how the real world works, it does not always operate this way. That's because it is a *general principle* rather than an *absolute truth*. Yes, generally it's true that when we sow good actions, we reap positive results. Conversely, it's also generally true that when we sow bad actions, we reap negative results. However, another saying is occasionally true even though it contradicts this one. That saying is "no good deed goes unpunished." This implies that good actions do not always yield fruitful results.

I'm not sharing these two opposing idioms to create confusion. Instead, I want to highlight something you probably already know but may not think about too often. Some general principles frequently prove to be true in the real world, but this does not mean they are always true. In this case, "you reap what you sow" is most often how the real world works. However, it doesn't always work that way. Occasionally, "no good deed goes unpunished" proves to be true instead.

In the same way, this is why I say E+R=O is how the real world works (or at least how it works best). While E+R=O is always a better approach than E=O, this doesn't mean you will always experience positive results with E+R=O. If, for instance, you work for an organization that lacks integrity, you might face backlash for practicing E+R=O. When this happens, is embracing an E=O mentality a good idea? Absolutely not! E=O is never a good idea because it causes you to surrender control to things outside of your control (i.e., *events)*. It is always better to live E+R=O, even when the real world doesn't work this way, because at the very least, it allows you to take ownership of your response. And when you own your response, you can grow, learn, and get better no matter what circumstances you face or what outcomes you achieve.

Here's one more thought about how the real world works (or at least how it works best). People who live according to values and priorities that are true, honorable, good, and virtuous typically experience the best outcomes in life. And this isn't just true for individuals—it applies to teams, organizations, companies, and even societies. Why? Because what is true, honorable, good, and virtuous constitutes the foundation for effective living and lasting happiness.

However, it's also true that the real world doesn't always work this way. When people, organizations, or societies live according to deficient, corrupt, and empty values, the real world does not work best. It becomes fractured, dysfunctional, and broken, rather than healthy and thriving.

All of these factors explain why E+R=O is how the real world works (or at least how it works best).

A second random thought is it's not too late for you to learn E+R=O. I speak on E+R=O to professional audiences everywhere, and I've had hundreds of conversations with people who say they wish they had learned this mindset earlier in life, just as I did. Some even ask, "Is it too late for me?"

Definitely not! It's never too late to live E+R=O.

In fact, believing it's too late indicates that you're thinking with an E=O mindset. What you're saying is, "Since I didn't learn E+R=O earlier in my life (*event*), I am now incapable of experiencing the benefits of E+R=O (*outcome*)." Don't think this way! Instead, remember what we discussed earlier. We cannot change what has been written in our lives—that ink is already dry. We can, however, take 100 percent responsibility for what is yet to be written. That ink is still in our pens. Whether you are 18 or 81, you can choose E+R=O.

Finally, no one lives E+R=O at all times. It's impossible to do so because no one is perfect. Even the most resilient people slip into E=O occasionally. Case in point, I teach this stuff and still have to be on guard daily against E=O thinking. We'll discuss this further in later chapters, but for now, let's acknowledge this reality upfront. No one is superhuman. Even those who develop a strong E+R=O muscle occasionally slip into E=O thinking.

※ ※ ※ ※ ※

The Way We View Things Is the Way We Do Things

So, our perspective—our mental glasses—shapes every experience. Now that we've begun to clean our lenses, it's time to explore what success truly means and how E+R=O serves as its foundation. After all, before you can build a life of significance, you must define what it looks like.

Part 2

THE FOUNDATION FOR SUCCESS

CHAPTER 3:

WHAT IS SUCCESS?

Have you ever seen the Greatest Show on Earth—Ringling Bros. and Barnum & Bailey Circus? What's your favorite act? The clowns? Elephants? Tightrope walkers or trapeze artists? How about the human cannonball, who gets shot out of...you guessed it...a cannon?

It's hard to pick a favorite, but when it comes to animal acts, I think lions are the best. Or I should say lion tamers. As a child, these folks were superheroes to me. Who else but superheroes steps into a cage packed with flesh-eating beasts? And who else but superheroes dares to stick their heads in the mouths of wild animals?

If you've ever seen lion tamers perform, you probably noticed that they enter the cage with several pieces of equipment. They carry a whip. There is a pistol at their side. And oddly enough, they're holding a stool. The whip and pistol make sense. But the stool? Are they planning a coffee break or something?

Yet, according to experts, the stool is their most important tool. The theory is that when a trainer holds the stool by the back and thrusts it toward a lion, the animal tries to focus on all four legs simultaneously. Its inability to hone in on a single leg overwhelms the lion, making it docile and somewhat paralyzed.[1]

THE MAIN THING

For everything we've discussed so far to truly work, we need to define what success looks like—and how E+R=O is central to achieving it.

Author and leadership expert Stephen Covey, whom I introduced in Chapter One, famously said, "The main thing is to keep the main thing the main thing."[2] Yet when it comes to success, most people have no idea what the "main thing" is. Instead of a clear definition, their vision is as fragmented as a lion trying to focus on all four legs of a stool at once.

If it sounds like I know what I'm talking about, it's because I do. For years, I chased success even though I was clueless about what it was or how to achieve it. For instance, like a lion, my vision bounced from one idea to another, including things like:

Prosperity—The feature most often associated with success is the acquisition of wealth. But money doesn't make someone successful—it simply amplifies their character, whether good or bad. Think about it: there are just as many dysfunctional, joyless people with money as there are fulfilled, joyful people without it. This is why prosperity is such a poor indicator of true success.

Prestige — In today's celebrity-driven culture, many people equate success with notoriety or fame. Yet we all know famous people whose lives are so messed up, we'd never trade places with them. So, how can fame possibly equal success?

Position — Having a position of power, prominence, or prestige is sometimes seen as the pinnacle of success. However, holding an important position is similar to having a lot of money. It can be used for good or bad, and usually it only amplifies a person's true character. So again, this makes for a poor benchmark of success.

Pleasure — The pursuit of pleasure is a central theme in modern culture, and who doesn't want to be happy and feel good? However, pleasure alone does not lead to lasting happiness. Indeed, it often results in feelings of emptiness. Although there is nothing fundamentally wrong with pleasure, true joy originates from things like meaningful relationships and the pursuit of worthwhile goals. By contrast, pleasure is fleeting and can be devoid of meaning. This is why pleasure is not a good definition of success.

Performance — "When I achieve this goal, then I will be successful." Have you ever thought this way? I certainly have. Frankly, this was my primary measure of success for a long time. However, I've discovered that each time I achieve a specific goal, the goalposts are moved either by me or someone else. This means success is always out of my reach. Please don't misunderstand; I strive for excellence in everything I do, and there is deep satisfaction in achieving noteworthy milestones. However, making performance your ultimate measure of success is disastrous. For one, as just mentioned, it means success always eludes you. But two, what happens if you cannot achieve your goals because of a lack of talent, or worse, because opportunities are taken away? Are you doomed to live a meaningless life? Again, I'm not saying accomplishing worthwhile goals is bad. Achieving goals is a good thing; a very good thing! However, basing your definition of success solely on performance is not.

While none of the things just listed are inherently wrong, they do not make for good definitions of success. And although defining true success in just a few short paragraphs is unrealistic (entire books have been written on the subject), we can identify at least one core element that Stephen Covey would say is "the main thing." He puts it this way: "Begin with the end in mind." He then states, "If you carefully consider what you want said of you at your funeral, you'll find your definition of success."[3]

Did you get that?

According to Covey, if you want a solid definition of success, think about what you want said about you at your funeral. Who will speak? What good, honorable, and noble things will they say about you? Will it be a celebration of a life well-lived or a dry ceremony filled with empty platitudes? In essence, imagine what you want the handful of people who know you best to say about you. Then, script out those comments in detail, and you'll have your definition of success.

For a bit more clarity, consider a word picture that New York Times columnist David Brooks uses in his book *The Road to Character*. He makes a distinction between "resume virtues" and "eulogy virtues." Resume virtues are the "skills you bring to the job market." By contrast, eulogy virtues "exist at the core of your being."[4] Notice the language Brooks uses here. Resume virtues are *skills*—things you can do. Eulogy virtues are *core* qualities—character traits that represent who you are. You need the first to be successful in your career, but you need the second to be successful in life.

Whatever analogy you choose, here's the key: Once you clarify your vision of success, you must bring that vision into reality. To borrow two phrases from my keynote presentations, you must *live it forward* and *move from dream to do* in your daily life. And you must do this today, tomorrow, the next day, the next month, and the next year. That is how you achieve success.

Again, according to Covey, "By keeping that end clearly in mind, you can make certain that whatever you do on any particular day does not violate the criteria you have defined as supremely important, and that each day of your life contributes in a meaningful way to the vision you have of your life as a whole."[5] Or, using Brooks' word picture, while you are busy earning a living by building your resume virtues, don't forget to stay true to your eulogy virtues so that you also create a meaningful life.

In summary, the best definition of success is to decide what good, virtuous, and honorable things you want said about you at your funeral. Once you clarify this, then live it forward into that definition, regardless of what events may come your way (i.e., E+R=O). Do this every day, and you'll build a solid foundation for success. Indeed, if you *truly* do this (not perfectly, but to the best of your ability), you'll be successful no matter how much money you make, what positions you hold, or whether you are famous or not.

YOUR COMPASS

A television program that aired right before the 1988 Winter Olympics featured skiers who were blind. Yes, you read that correctly—blind skiers.

As crazy as it sounds, these individuals were trained to be slalom skiers. Each was paired with a sighted skier, and initially, they were taught how to make turns on bunny slopes. Once turns were mastered, they were taken to the slalom slopes. As they skied down these slopes, their sighted partners skied right beside them, calling out commands: "Left!" "Right!" Eventually, these blind skiers learned to navigate slalom courses relying solely on the words of their sighted partners. Talk about trust![6]

Wouldn't it be great if we had a trusted advisor traveling alongside us? Someone or something to guide us through life with clear, reliable directions? Someone or something that reminds us to stay the course, especially when we face rugged terrain?

Well, we can have such a trusted advisor.

It's called a personal purpose statement.

If you are unsure of the role a personal purpose statement plays, it's sort of like a sighted skier who helps you navigate life. Better yet, think of it as a *compass* you can carry with you that always points to true north and reminds you how you want to live your life.[7]

When I first launched my company, *Live It Forward*, it focused primarily on career coaching and training. In those early years, one of the core exercises we did with every client was to help them create a personal purpose statement. Initially, the process was complicated. It was more akin to drafting a cumbersome constitution than a simple compass. Eventually, however, we figured out a better method based on the following criteria:

Portable — A purpose statement must be short enough to "carry it around with you." If your statement is too long (like a constitution), you'll have difficulty memorizing it and won't be able to access it in those critical moments when you need it most.

Expandable — One problem, however, with a short purpose statement is that if it's written superficially, it won't be effective. For example, if your life's purpose is "to do good with the talents I have," then your statement isn't much more than a feel-good sentiment. Yes, it meets the first condition of being portable, but what does it really say? For a short, portable statement to function like a compass, it also needs to be expandable. This means it should be written in such a way that it relates to each of the most important roles in your life.

Personal — This third criterion is often the most challenging. As with the example just mentioned, people frequently create generic purpose statements such as "to do good with the talents I have." Notice how this statement applies to almost anyone because it doesn't specify any particular talents or their applications. Yet the reason a personal purpose statement is called "personal" is because it must be specific to you. It cannot be generic. That means you must write your purpose statement so others cannot copy it and paste it into their lives. It has to be personal to you.

Aspirational — Finally, your purpose statement should articulate who you aspire to be on your best days. Will you live this out perfectly? No. But do you aspire to live this way each and every day? Absolutely!

THE THREE BIGGIES

Using the criteria just listed as your guide for creating a portable, expandable, personal, and aspirational purpose statement, you're now ready to craft your own statement by answering three key questions. These questions are easy to understand but challenging to answer. Why? Because they are three of the biggest questions you can ask yourself about life.

- **The "One Thing" Question** — If you boiled life down to a single truth or philosophy that makes life meaningful and valuable (and you must force yourself to choose just one), what is it?
- **The "Being" Question** — How will your One Thing shape your Being? In other words, how will it influence who you are at your core, and how will it shape your character, morals, and values (i.e., eulogy virtues)?
- **The "Doing" Question** — Once you determine how your One Thing shapes your Being, how will these two elements impact your Doing (i.e., resume virtues)?

As I said, these questions are easy to understand but tough to answer. However, by objectively answering them, you are well on your way to defining what success means to you. In fact, did you notice how these questions help you answer what good, virtuous, and noble things you want said about you at your funeral? That's because they get to the heart and soul of who you are and how you want to live.

And speaking of who you are and how you want to live, here's one last crucial point to remember: we are human *beings*, not human doings. In other words, our doing flows out of our being. If you want to accomplish good, honorable, and virtuous things in your life, you must start by being a good, honorable, and virtuous person. This doesn't mean you have to be perfect, but it does mean you must pursue a high standard of character.

In light of all this, here's a small sampling of purpose statements from some of my former clients. These should be seen as examples only, not as something to copy and paste into your life. Remember, a personal purpose statement is called "personal" because it should be unique to you.

Additionally, I include notes in parentheses so that you can clearly see how each client answered the three big questions. These notes are guideposts for you to follow; they're not part of each person's purpose statements.

> **Example 1:** (One Thing) To remain optimistic and hopeful no matter what life brings my way (Being) by being humble, generous, kind, and joyful, (Doing) and by advising and leading others to persistently find positive solutions so that they can accomplish their goals with excellence.

> **Example 2:** (One Thing) To honor God and faithfully serve Him (Being) by being a leader who (Doing) inspires and equips others to live intentionally and proactively in what matters most.

Example 3: (One Thing) To enjoy life and live it to the fullest (Being) while being so full of joy that it spills over on to every person I meet, (Doing) and to empower family, friends, and customers to have fun and live life to the fullest as well.

Example 4: (One Thing) To experience real joy and happiness (Being) by being a good husband, son, brother, and friend, (Doing) and by serving animals who are suffering.

Example 5: (One Thing) To walk confidently with God (Being) so that I live my daily life with strength and balance, (Doing) and to use my talents as a communicator, learner, and problem solver to serve and strengthen people and organizations.[8]

You can download a free Purpose Statement Worksheet at **KENTJULIAN.COM/RESPONSEBOOK**. This simple resource will help you craft your personal purpose statement.

IN AND OUT OF SEASON

Finally, there is one more test to ensure that your purpose statement can endure over time—it needs to be reliable both in and out of season.

What do I mean by "in and out of season"?

In and out of season means your purpose statement represents your core beliefs, regardless of what's happening in the world, and no matter what events you face. That is to say, it doesn't matter if:

- Circumstances are favorable or unfavorable
- Obstacles are major or minor
- Culture agrees with you or not

Therefore, if your purpose statement objectively points to true north despite what is happening around you, that's a great indicator that your compass will guide you toward excellence, achievement, and success in what is true, noble, good, and honorable.

But don't forget, now you must live it forward. You must lean into your purpose statement daily—the good, honorable, true, and virtuous *being* and *doing* qualities that you have predetermined are most important to you. If you do this, there's a good chance you'll be successful regardless of how much money you earn, what positions you attain, or whether you become well-known or not.

★ ★ ★ ★ ★

> Now that we understand that success isn't found in outcomes alone—but in how we live, lead, and respond—we're ready to explore how we can expand our lives (or, if we're not careful, how we might shrink our lives).

CHAPTER 4:

THE EXPANDING FENCE POSTS

BELIEVE IT OR NOT, my first real career was lifeguarding.

Yes, I said "real."

Before you start in with the *Baywatch* wisecracks, let me explain.

What began as a summer job eventually led to managing numerous pools, leading multiple staff teams, coaching several championship swim teams, certifying hundreds of new employees, and being offered a vice president position seven years later at a large and growing company.

But…

None of this would have come about if I had been fired.

Which almost happened.

ALMOST TERMINATED

After my junior year of high school, I became a lifeguard for the same reason many teenagers do—I thought it would be a cool summer job. During that summer, however, I learned that a positive opportunity can turn negative when you're irresponsible. In this case, the positive opportunity was being hired by a small but growing company. How did things turn negative? Near the end of the summer, the company owner pulled me off the lifeguard stand and almost fired me on the spot. Why? Because I had failed to grasp the seriousness of my job. My focus was on getting a tan and flirting with girls; it should have been on protecting lives.

Looking back, I have no idea why Mr. Legg (yes, that was his real name) didn't fire me. Here's how bad my conduct was:

- I lifeguarded at one of the largest pools in the Atlanta suburbs. It was not unusual for 150 to 200 people—most of them children—to be in the pool at once.
- Community board members complained multiple times about my job performance.
- After numerous complaints, Mr. Legg decided to stop by and see for himself. He sat quietly at a corner table to watch me in action.
- For 30 minutes, he witnessed an employee who never once altered his tanning and flirting behavior, even though his boss was sitting right there.

When Mr. Legg asked me to step down from the lifeguard stand, he laid into me. He kept his composure and remained professional, but the conversation was incredibly uncomfortable. What angered him most, and rightfully so, was that I never once glanced at the shallow end of the pool. If you've never lifeguarded, it might surprise you that most drownings occur in the shallow end. That's because this is where all the young, inexperienced swimmers hang out. And here I was, the clueless lifeguard, ignoring the most dangerous section of the pool.

Again, I have no idea why Mr. Legg didn't terminate me; he had a reputation for firing people immediately for mistakes like mine. But I'm thankful he didn't because that conversation set me straight. It's embarrassing to admit, but up until that point, my poor performance hadn't dawned on me. Yet, in that moment, I knew he was right. So, instead of making excuses, I started to attack my job with a new mindset. Here's how things changed:

- When I began my second year with the company, I was on probation. By the end of that summer, however, my conduct had improved so much that Mr. Legg promoted me to head lifeguard at the company's largest pool.
- The following year, I was promoted to pool manager and also became a swim coach.
- At the end of that year, our pool won the first of three consecutive "Pool of the Summer" awards. This was a contest between all the pools our company managed. Amazingly, the same board members who had reported my bad behavior just a few years earlier were now enthusiastically voting for my staff and me to win this award.

- By year four, I was managing multiple pools, interviewing dozens of summer staff, certifying most of the company's new lifeguards, and even coaching a championship swim team.
- When I graduated from college and began searching for work in a different career, Mr. Legg offered me one of the company's two vice president positions. It paid considerably more than the non-profit job I ultimately accepted, so I was tempted. However, since it didn't align with my vocational calling, I turned it down.

A WAKE-UP CALL

Most people don't view lifeguarding as a real career, which I understand. I didn't view it that way either when I started in this line of work. Like I said, I just wanted to get a tan and flirt with girls.

Nevertheless, I don't know of any other job that could have given me a stronger foundation for success. Working for this company introduced me to virtually every professional skill I've used in both nonprofit and for-profit leadership. Leading teams. Hiring and firing employees. Managing facilities. Cultivating corporate culture. Engaging with and training staff. Marketing and sales. Customer service. Working with boards. Even media relations and interviews.

But more importantly, my first year with the company was a tipping point for me. It served as a wake-up call. You see, I had been introduced to the concept of E+R=O in middle school and had successfully applied it to a few areas of my life. However, I was compartmentalizing it. I used it like an emergency cord—pulling it whenever I was in trouble. I hadn't yet realized that E+R=O could be the foundation for success in all areas of my life.

Additionally, I hadn't realized that being Response-ABLE goes a step beyond being responsible. Whereas being responsible implies doing what is expected of you (which, of course, is a good thing), being Response-ABLE means you take 100 percent ownership of your response in *all* circumstances. It means consciously choosing your response in both good and bad situations. Most importantly, it means living according to predetermined values and priorities rather than letting your emotions and feelings drive your behavior.

BE LIKE EINSTEIN

Looking back, the reason I hadn't integrated E+R=O into all areas of my life is because I hadn't simplified it enough.

You might be scratching your head and wondering, "Didn't you earlier compare E+R=O to a multifaceted sapphire? How can something be multifaceted yet simple at the same time? That sounds contradictory."

I agree, it does sound contradictory...even confusing.

But honestly, it's not.

On the surface, describing E+R=O as "multifaceted" might make it seem complicated. However, when we study a concept in depth to understand it more thoroughly, this doesn't necessarily imply that the concept becomes more complex. It actually implies the opposite. It indicates that we are moving away from a naive and superficial view of the idea and toward something more robust and solid. Furthermore—and this is important—as we develop a deeper understanding of a concept, we discover that there is simplicity on both the front end and back end of our knowledge. Allow me to retype that sentence so that you can reread it and think about it more deeply: As we develop a deeper understanding of a concept, we discover that there is simplicity on both the *front end* and *back end* of our knowledge.

To better wrap your head around this idea, consider what Oliver Wendell Holmes Sr. said: "For the simplicity on this side of complexity, I wouldn't give you a fig. But for the simplicity on the other side of complexity, for that I would give you anything I have."[1] So what does "simplicity on the other side of complexity" mean? And what makes it so valuable?

This phrase refers to a deeper, more meaningful understanding that emerges only when we move beyond our initial assumptions about a concept, task, or problem. In other words, the more we learn, the more clarity we gain. As a result, our understanding not only becomes more accurate, but also more profound.

Eventually, we move past the naive simplicity we started with and arrive at a richer, more thorough simplicity. You might even call it a *truer* simplicity. The value of this journey toward a truer simplicity is illustrated by the three stages of a bell curve:

Stage 1: Naive Simplicity. At the beginning of learning or trying something new, our understanding tends to be simplistic. It's based on surface-level assumptions and incomplete information. We are still novices who are unaware of what we don't know.

Stage 2: Increased Complexity. As we gain knowledge and experience, we inevitably encounter challenges that expose the limits of our initial understanding. This stage can feel confusing or overwhelming, but it's essential. It's what pushes us to ask better questions, rethink our assumptions, and develop a more nuanced perspective.

Stage 3: Simplicity on the Other Side of Complexity. With time, learning, and reflection, our understanding becomes deeper and better informed. We've done the hard work of wrestling with complexity, and now we're able to communicate essential truths with clarity and confidence.

This *Simplicity Bell Curve* offers a powerful framework for understanding the journey required to achieve mastery and expertise in any subject. Interestingly, it also mirrors the way Albert Einstein approached thinking and problem-solving.

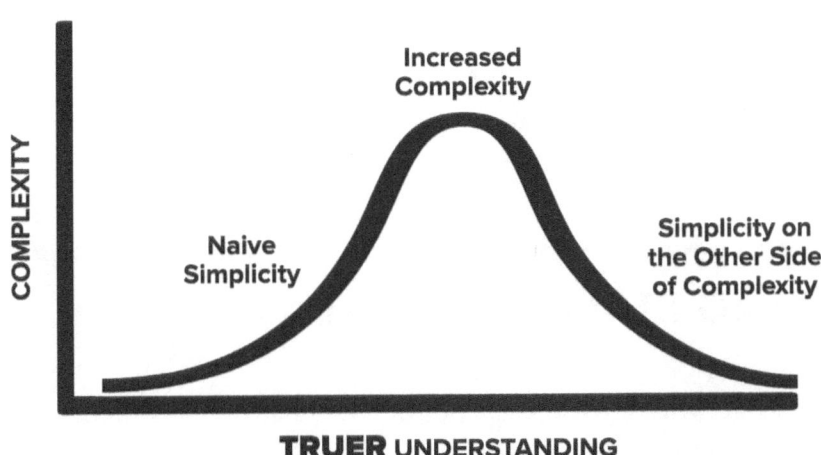

When people think of Einstein, most think of the man with funny hair who discovered the theory of relativity ($E=mc^2$). They describe him with words like "brilliant," "genius," and even "brainiac." Few, however, use the word "simple." Yet, according to Einstein, "Genius is making complex ideas simple, not making simple ideas complex." He also said, "Everything should be made as simple as possible, but not simpler." And, "If you can't explain it simply, you don't understand it well enough."[2] Each of these statements highlights the fact that Einstein was a simplifier, which was a significant factor for his brilliance.

Similarly, we would be wise to make E+R=O as simple as possible, but not any simpler. To achieve this, however, we must move beyond a basic knowledge of the mindset and toward a more robust and comprehensive understanding.

With this in mind, I'd like to introduce you to a core tool I developed years ago called the *4 Fence Posts of Being Response-ABLE*. As outlined in the Simplicity Bell Curve, I believe the following three images can guide us from a naive simplicity to a deeper, more informed understanding of the essential truths of E+R=O. Furthermore, they reveal how the mindset we choose either empowers or limits our success.

4 FENCE POSTS OF BEING RESPONSE-ABLE

Let's start with a basic snapshot of the 4 Fence Posts themselves. The following image depicts a person's life via a four-sided fence. On the corners are four posts, each representing an area for which a person is 100 percent Response-ABLE. No one else is in charge of these four areas, so it's up to each individual to choose how they will respond. For instance:

Attitude — No matter what events occur in your life, you and you alone own your attitude. You are in charge.

Associations — You are the only one who chooses the associations that influence your life. For one, you determine *who* you associate with and *how* you interact with them. Two, you also discern *what* content you allow into your mind and heart. All of these are your choices. You might argue that you cannot choose your work associates or family. I'll grant you that. However, you still determine how you interact with these individuals and how you allow them to influence you. Again, you are in charge.

Articulation — You alone decide what words proceed from your mouth. You have complete control over what you say to other people and yourself. Here again, you are in charge.

Actions — No matter what happens to you, you are 100 percent responsible for your actions. Once more, you are in charge.

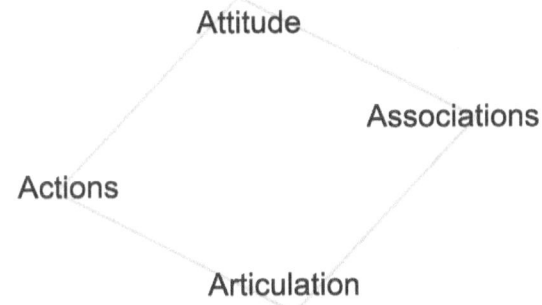

THE EQUATION THAT ALWAYS ADDS UP

When you embrace an E+R=O mindset and choose to be Response-ABLE, you take ownership of your life. Instead of allowing events, which are mostly out of your control, to determine your outcomes, you aim to shape your outcomes through how you respond to them. You intentionally live it forward instead of reacting impulsively. You strive to live according to predetermined values and priorities rather than being ruled by feelings and emotions.

Will you respond correctly every time? Of course not. But instead of being a victim of circumstances beyond your control (or even your own mistakes), you know that you can pivot and make wiser choices next time. Therefore, you accept responsibility and learn from each experience. You grow and become stronger. And as you mature, your ability to handle difficult situations improves.

While all of this is happening, you start to notice something. As demonstrated in the image below, *your life expands*. More opportunities open up for you. New roles and responsibilities present themselves. Others start asking for your opinions and insights. All of this occurs because people recognize you are strong. You are not someone who crumbles in the face of adversity. You are someone others can count on. You have character. You are trustworthy. You are Response-ABLE.

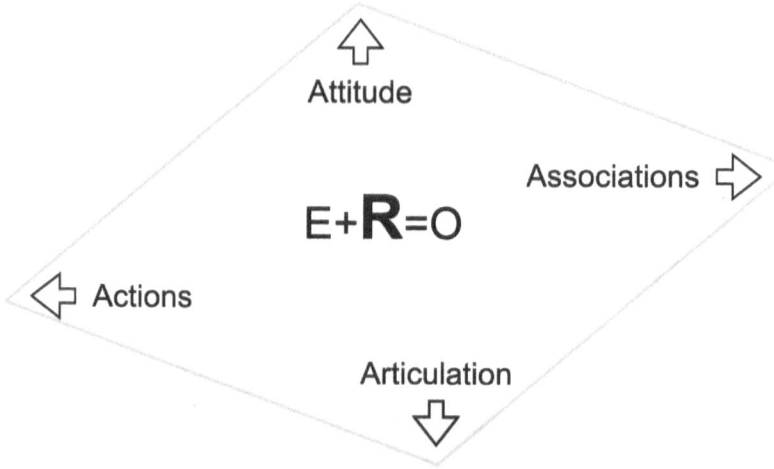

THE EQUATION THAT ALWAYS TAKES AWAY

The exact opposite happens if you have an E=O mentality. Instead of taking ownership of your life, you become a victim who allows events to determine your outcomes. Instead of being Response-ABLE, you react impulsively. And rather than living by predetermined values and priorities, you are driven by your feelings and emotions.

Additionally, when facing adversities, instead of learning and growing, you fall apart. You blame, bully, and bulldoze people. You also avoid accepting responsibility, so instead of maturing and getting better, you regress and become bitter. And as shown in the image below, the longer you live this way, the more *your life shrinks*. Opportunities disappear. New roles don't present themselves. And no one is interested in your opinions.

Amazingly, while you blame circumstances or other people, the primary reason this is happening to you is *you*. You are living E=O. Every time you face adversity, you crumble. You are a person of weak character. You are neither trustworthy nor dependable. As a result, people have little respect for you.

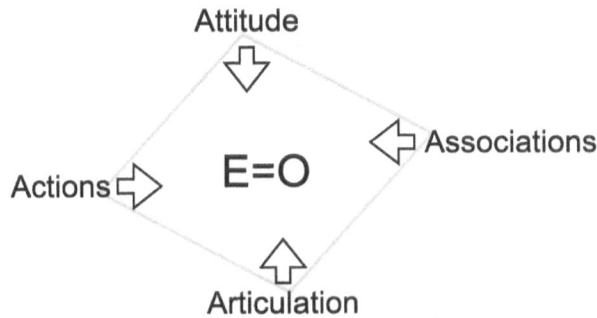

To reiterate, these three images have proven to be the simplest yet most profound tool in my E+R=O toolbox. I have used them with middle school and high school students, teachers and college professors, athletes, frontline workers, government employees, business professionals, and CEOs. And to a person, everyone gets it. They *all* understand the concept. That's because these images capture the essence of how an E+R=O mindset versus an E=O mindset impacts our lives.

One last thing before wrapping up this chapter. Although the E=O explanation I just shared sounds harsh, it reflects reality. No matter how today's culture tries to redefine things, this is how the real world operates (or at least how it operates best). So when I state this truth, even if it's uncomfortable to hear, it doesn't come from a lack of care or concern. In fact, it's the exact opposite. I'm being so direct because I care! E+R=O causes a person's life to expand. Yet E=O pulls a person in the other direction—it causes that person's life to shrink. The sooner someone realizes this, the sooner they can add the R to their life and start building their foundation for success.

THE REST OF THE STORY (AGAIN)

As with my story about middle school basketball, I need to share the rest of the story about lifeguarding. Like the first story, this experience gave me an incredible gift. This second gift moved me from being a novice of E+R=O toward a deeper, more profound understanding.

As mentioned, when I started working for the pool company, I was familiar with the basics of E+R=O. However, I lacked consistency. I was hit or miss at applying the mindset. Furthermore, I only used E+R=O when I faced obstacles. When things were good, I didn't think about being Response-ABLE.

Do you see how immature this is? I was like a child who saw E+R=O as an emergency cord to pull whenever I was in danger. And while this approach helped me navigate some adversities, I was missing the bigger picture. I overlooked the fact that E+R=O could be my foundation for success at *all* times, not just during tough times.

This is why almost getting fired served as a wake-up call for me. After that first year, I started to navigate my way through the Simplicity Bell Curve. During the next six years in that job, I applied E+R=O to every obstacle and *opportunity* I faced. As I did, my understanding grew more robust and useful. I progressed from a naive simplicity to a more thorough, truer simplicity. Even better, that seven-year journey played a key role in the eventual creation of the most valuable tool in my E+R=O toolbox—the 4 Fence Posts of Being Response-ABLE.

The greatest eye-opening moment for me came at the end of my time with this company. In his direct, matter-of-fact manner, Mr. Legg said to me, "If someone had told me after your first year that you would be one of the best leaders working for my company…that I would try to hire you as a vice president…there is no way I would have believed that person. I usually fire people on the spot for what you did. I don't know why I didn't fire you, but I'm glad I didn't."

I'm glad he didn't either!

★ ★ ★ ★ ★

Clearly, your beliefs are fence posts that either box you in or help you move forward. Next, let's broaden our perspective by exploring how E+R=O ties all success principles together. What you'll discover is that E+R=O doesn't compete with other personal growth ideas—it completes them.

CHAPTER 5:

IT'S A BIG UMBRELLA!

HERE'S AN UNUSUAL CRIME. Thieves broke into a store and inadvertently triggered the alarm system. Lucky for them, they slipped out into the darkness before getting caught.

Later, when the store owner met with the police at the crime scene, he was relieved to discover nothing had been stolen. "Yes! My alarm system actually worked."

The next day, however, a man came to the checkout counter with a suit priced at $5. Someone else approached with a plastic bracelet marked $450. A designer dress—$2.75. A pair of flip-flops—$295. It eventually dawned on the staff that the thieves didn't break in to steal anything. They simply switched the price tags.[1]

WHY E+R=O IS THE FOUNDATION FOR SUCCESS

In the first section of this book, "A Picture of Reality," we defined E+R=O (*Events + RESPONSE = Outcome*). After doing that, we learned that E+R=O is how the real world works (or at least how it works best).

In this second part, "The Foundation for Success," we have been exploring the role E+R=O plays in success. So far, we have answered two questions. In Chapter Three, we answered the question "*What is success?*" and discovered the best way to define success is to begin with the end in mind by predetermining what we want said about us at our funeral. Next, in Chapter Four, we examined "*How* does E+R=O enable success?" and found that E+R=O is the equation that expands our life, while E=O is the one that shrinks it.

Before transitioning to the third part of the book, "The Muscle Behind Grit," we need to ask one more important question. The answer reveals the most critical connection between E+R=O and success because it unifies everything we've learned so far about personal growth and success. The question is: "*Why* is E+R=O the foundation for success?" To answer this question, we'll examine two key terms, followed by 10 general truths.

TWO KEY TERMS

Let's start with defining two key terms. You'll probably recognize them from the previous chapters, but we need to ensure we have a crystal-clear understanding of each: *principles* and *mindset*.

PRINCIPLES

According to Vocabulary.com, principles are "standards of good behavior" and "basic truths that help you with your life." This is why, in Chapter Two, I described principles as fundamental truths rather than absolute truths. Although principles reliably predict how things generally work in the real world, they don't guarantee things will always work out that way. To demonstrate this, we examined two well-known expressions—"you reap what you sow" and "no good deed goes unpunished." The first reflects how the real world usually operates. However, as we found out, there are times when the second one turns out to be true instead.

Stephen Covey offers additional insight here. He describes principles as "natural laws" that act as "guidelines for human conduct that are proven to have enduring, permanent value. They're fundamental."[2] He also explains that principles are "essentially unarguable because they are self-evident. One way to quickly grasp the self-evident nature of principles is to simply consider the absurdity of attempting to live an effective life based on their opposites. I doubt that anyone would seriously consider unfairness, deceit, baseness, uselessness, mediocrity, or degeneration to be a solid foundation for lasting happiness or success."[3] This is why I suggested that when individuals, teams, organizations, companies, and even societies live according to unethical or corrupt values, the "real world" stops working as it should—it becomes fractured, dysfunctional, and broken.

MINDSET

Vocabulary.com defines mindset as "a habitual mental attitude that determines how you interpret and respond to situations." That is to say, our mindset influences the way we live our lives and how we choose to handle different situations.

Again, you might recall that I used the analogy of lenses to explain a person's mindset and stated, "The way we view things is the way we do things." For this reason, when our mindset is E=O, we see life through upside-down lenses and mistakenly believe our outcomes depend solely on events or circumstances.

However, when we choose the right-side-up lenses of E+R=O, we gain a different perspective. Events still influence our outcomes, but they don't play an exclusive role in determining them. Our responses also affect our outcomes. And our responses, more often than not, have a greater impact on the outcomes we experience.

WHY THIS MATTERS

The reason for thoroughly defining these two words is that, without understanding their differences, you might miss one of the most important correlations between E+R=O and success: E+R=O is a *mindset*, not a *principle*.

This matters because the word mindset is fundamentally different from the word principle. Your mindset refers to something *inside* of you that is *unique* to you. It is your particular, internal way of perceiving things. Conversely, a principle refers to a general truth that exists *outside* of you and is *universal* to everyone. It is a common, external law that serves as a guideline for conduct.

This brings us back to the original question from the start of the chapter: "*Why* is E+R=O the foundation for success?"

Put simply, E+R=O is the foundation for success because it is the mindset that gets success principles working for you instead of against you.

Don't miss what was just written.

E+R=O is the *mindset* (the unique, inner lenses through which you view things) that gets success *principles* (the natural laws outside of you that are universal to everyone) working for you instead of against you.

I'll explain what I mean by "getting success principles working for you instead of against you" by the end of this chapter, but for now, let's make sure we're clear on the following:

- E+R=O is *not* a principle.
- E+R=O *is* a mindset.

While it might seem like I'm hammering a minor point, it's crucial not to confuse these two words. Again, as a mindset, E+R=O is a unique, internal set of lenses that shapes how you see the world. These lenses operate from the inside out, meaning the more you embrace an E+R=O mindset, the more you align your life with external, fundamental principles that have proven to be enduring, valuable, noble, and good. In other words, if you view life through E+R=O lenses (i.e., mindset), you ground yourself in the fundamental laws (i.e., principles) of how the real world works (or at least how it works best).

Think of it like this: E+R=O is an umbrella under which all success principles fall. The idiom "falling under one umbrella" refers to how various items can be grouped under a single, overarching theme. For instance, firefighters, paramedics, and emergency room technicians all fall under the umbrella of Emergency Medical Services (EMS). In the same way, all success principles fall under the umbrella of E+R=O because E+R=O is the mindset necessary to live out *every* success principle.

Incidentally, that's why the cover of this book has a line drawn through the phrase "most important" and replaces it with the word "only." E+R=O is not the most important mindset for success—it is the *only* mindset for success. It is the one and only mindset under which all success principles fall!

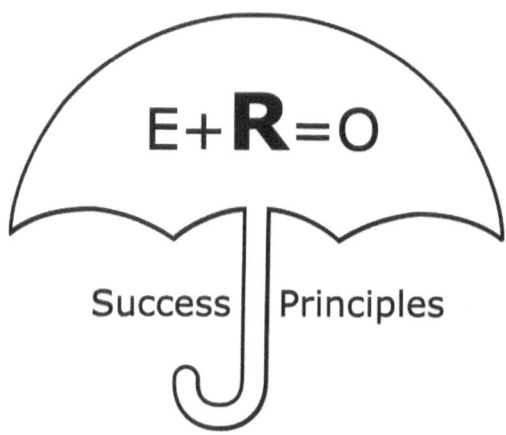

This leads us to the 10 general truths I promised to share. These truths will shed more light on the answer to the question: "*Why* is E+R=O the foundation for success?" That's because each truth is a success principle (10 of my favorites), and together they illustrate how all success principles fall under the E+R=O umbrella.

THE E+R=O UMBRELLA

PRINCIPLE 1:
BIG IS LITTLE AND LITTLE IS BIG

Let's start with one of my favorite success principles.

Most people want to experience the big things life has to offer. Meaningful relationships, a career they enjoy, the ability to earn a good living, and opportunities to make a positive impact—just to name a few. Yet the secret to experiencing big successes is counterintuitive to what most people think. Instead of hoping for a big break or a big score, individuals who most often succeed typically do so by taking little, important steps day in and day out. And it's these small steps, when taken consistently, that eventually lead to big successes.

Do you know what gives you the resilience to keep taking small, essential steps, especially when life gets tough? An E+R=O mindset!

BIG is little and little is BIG.

PRINCIPLE 2:
YOUR DOING FLOWS FROM YOUR BEING

This principle reminds us that who we are on the inside shapes how we behave on the outside.

For example, if integrity is one of your core values, you will most often tell the truth. Furthermore, when you do lie, your conscience will bother you enough that you either admit you lied or at least avoid similar lies in the future. By contrast, if you are not a person of integrity, lying will be second nature to you.

So, how does an E+R=O mindset get this success principle working for you instead of against you? Using the illustration just mentioned, let's say you're a habitual liar. Perhaps it started with little white lies, but over time, your lies have grown bigger and bolder. Things finally reach a flash point when you're caught lying multiple times about something significant. Trust erodes quickly, and you realize, perhaps for the first time, that your reputation could be broken beyond repair.

This is a watershed moment for you, one in which you choose to be Response-ABLE. The first thing you do is take full ownership of your deceit and apologize. Next, you seek to rectify the situation however possible. Finally, you get serious about becoming a person of integrity (i.e., your being). This includes creating an accountability structure, reading personal development books on integrity, and journaling about your struggles (i.e., your doing). You know the journey ahead won't be easy, but you're determined to break this bad habit and realize that E+R=O is the mindset needed to overcome your integrity problem.

Your DOING flows from your BEING.

PRINCIPLE 3:
HARD WORK BEATS TALENT WHEN TALENT DOESN'T WORK HARD

This is another one of my favorite success principles because I have witnessed its positive results time and again in my life.

As mentioned earlier, I'm not the sharpest tack in the box. Nor am I the brightest bulb in the chandelier. I'm poking fun at myself with these clichés, but the truth is, I don't have gobs of natural talent. I'm average at best. Yet this is precisely why E+R=O is such a game-changer. It can be an incredible equalizer in your life and career!

Think about it this way. Regardless of one's talent or skill level, if an individual is passionate about something, they are likely to work harder than other people. Eventually, they will outperform others who are more naturally gifted simply because they are willing to put in the sweat equity. That's why this success principle is such a great equalizer—it allows average people to perform at a higher level than their more gifted counterparts.

Hard work beats talent when talent doesn't work hard.

PRINCIPLE 4:
DO THE OPPOSITE

Success is simple. The secret? Do the opposite of what most people do, and you will be successful.

For instance, most people hit the snooze button as soon as they wake up. When they finally get out of bed, they scarf down breakfast before rushing out the door. Upon arriving at work, they invest as little effort as possible and blame problems on circumstances or other people. When they get home, instead of investing in the relationships they claim matter most, they spend hours vegging out in front of the TV or scrolling through their mobile devices. They go to bed exhausted and wake up the next morning only to repeat this process all over again.

Rather than taking this approach, what would happen if you did the opposite? What if you woke up earlier than most and dedicated 20 minutes to reading? What if you gave your best effort at work and then scheduled 30 minutes for exercise before heading home? And what if, upon arriving home, you carved out time to invest in your most important relationships? How different would your life be if you didn't do what "normal" people do?

Don't miss this—all the actions listed in the previous paragraph are E+R=O actions. No exceptional talent needed. Merely a willingness to do the opposite of what most people do. As Jodie Foster said, "Normal is not something to aspire to; it's something to get away from."[4] Success is simple. Do the opposite.

PRINCIPLE 5: HABITS MAKE YOU OR BREAK YOU

Brian Tracy writes, "The fact is that good habits are hard to form, but easy to live with. Bad habits, on the other hand, are easy to form, but hard to live with. In either case, you develop either good or bad habits as the result of your choices, decisions, and behaviors."[5]

The correlation between E+R=O and this success principle is pretty straightforward. An E+R=O mindset empowers you to be Response-ABLE, which leads to positive choices, decisions, and behaviors. Conversely, an E=O mindset causes you to run away from being Response-ABLE, which leads to poor choices, decisions, and behaviors.

Habits MAKE you or BREAK you. Guaranteed.

PRINCIPLE 6:
SUCCESS (AND FAILURE) LEAVE CLUES

Lots of people have big dreams, yet most never achieve them. Why is that? It's because figuring out how to move from dream to do can be difficult.

But you can figure this out, and it's not as hard as you think. If you know where to look, you'll see that success leaves clues.

For example, if there is something you want to learn to do, I guarantee that you can find dozens, hundreds, or even thousands of people who have already accomplished it. Many have written books, started podcasts, recorded videos, and created courses. Find these clues and take action!

Even better, you probably already know people who can help. What's stopping you from networking with these individuals? Years ago, when I struggled in school, I found teachers and friends who taught me how to study. Later, when starting my career, I networked with several successful professionals in my industry and learned from them. When I married Kathy and wanted to be the best husband I could be, I befriended older men who had great marriages. I did the same thing when I became a father. And this pattern has continued over the years in learning how to write books, start a business, become a professional speaker, and more.

Learning to move from dream to do by finding clues that successful people leave is the essence of an E+R=O mindset. Think about it—the *event* is you not knowing how to do something. The *outcome* you desire is to learn how to do that thing. What will move you from your current event to your desired outcome? Your *response* of finding clues and taking action. It's that simple!

As a side note, failure also leaves clues. That's why it's wise to identify behaviors and actions to avoid. Knowing what to steer clear of can be as valuable, if not more valuable, than finding the clues to follow.

Success (and failure) leave clues. Look for them!

PRINCIPLE 7:
THE PROBLEM IS NOT THE PROBLEM

One of my speaker friends, Scotty Sanders, frequently speaks about this success principle by saying, "What we think is the problem is not the real problem. The real problem is in how we are thinking about the problem."

Another great friend, Dan Miller, often said, "A problem is an opportunity looking for a solution." He would then state that the best question to ask when facing a dilemma is, "What does this make possible?" I love this! By asking this question, you immediately pivot away from solely focusing on the problem to considering your response. And when you do this, you quickly discover...

The problem is not the problem.

PRINCIPLE 8:
MORE IS LEARNED THROUGH MOVEMENT THAN MEDITATION

When our children were young, they loved using our electric pencil sharpener. Their goal? To get their pencil tip as sharp as possible. One by one, our three little kiddos would push their pencil into the sharpener for five to 10 seconds. If the tip wasn't perfectly pointed when they pulled it out, the pencil would be jammed back into the sharpener immediately.

Bzzz. Bzzz. Bzzz. Bzzz. Bzzz.

When I couldn't take it anymore, I'd snap. "Stop sharpening your pencils," I'd laughingly exclaim. Then, I gently reminded them that the pencil tip didn't need to be perfect to start writing.

Similarly, you and I can sabotage ourselves by thinking everything must be perfect before we start moving. Yet the very act of moving often teaches us more about what needs to be done than getting stuck meditating on how to make things perfect. Yes, there is a time for thinking and planning. But there also comes a time when we need to say, "Good enough is good enough—let's get moving."

As the saying goes, "Perfection is the enemy of progress." To achieve specific outcomes, stop waiting for everything to be perfect and start taking action. As you do, your E+R=O mindset will help you learn, grow, and adjust along the way.

More is learned through movement than meditation.

PRINCIPLE 9: MORE IS LEARNED THROUGH STRUGGLE THAN STRENGTH

Everyone wants life to be smooth sailing, but you cannot become a great sailor without learning to navigate storms. Therefore, when you face struggles, your main goal shouldn't only be to get through the trial—seek to learn *from* it as well.

By now, you probably know what I'm going to say. But in case you're wondering, here it is—E+R=O is the mindset that enables you to put this success principle into practice.

How?

By elevating your outlook in the midst of a trial.

Remember, E+R=O leads to learned optimism, which helps a person view tough events as temporary and specific rather than permanent and pervasive. As a result, even in the middle of painful storms, we can learn new lessons and gain new insights. And the truth is, pain is often a better teacher than comfort.

More is learned through struggle than strength.

PRINCIPLE 10: SHORTCUTS COST TOO MUCH

Lee Ellis endured over five years as a prisoner of war in Vietnam. In his book, *Leading With Honor*, he writes:

> *I learned that leading with honor is about doing the right thing, even when it entails personal sacrifice. More often than not, doing the right things—accepting responsibility, fulfilling your duty, telling the truth, and remaining faithful to your word—is the most difficult thing to do, but it's also the thing that brings long-term success. Shortcuts may work for the moment, but almost everything of lasting value comes at a price.*[6]

That's an E+R=O statement if there ever was one! As a prisoner of war, Ellis learned that he could be Response-ABLE even in the most dire of circumstances.

Let's be honest: there are no shortcuts to becoming a better person, developing meaningful relationships, achieving career success, or building wealth. Achieving anything worthwhile comes at a price, and it will likely cost you a lot. But that price will feel like pennies compared to the cost of taking shortcuts.

Shortcuts cost too much.

DON'T SWITCH THE PRICE TAGS

As we wrap up Part Two of this book, one final insight will tie a bow around why E+R=O is the foundation for success.

We have spent the last several chapters answering three questions that deepened our understanding of the role E+R=O plays in success. In Chapter Three, we examined the question "*What is success?*" which led us to define success and clarify the idea of purpose. In Chapter Four, we explored the question "*How does E+R=O enable success?*" and found that E+R=O expands our life while E=O shrinks it. In this chapter, we asked "*Why is E+R=O the foundation for success?*" and learned that it serves as the umbrella under which all success principles fall.

But there is something that I have left unsaid in this chapter. You may have picked up on it already, but it still needs to be stated aloud. Here it is…

Both E+R=O and E=O are umbrellas. That means all success principles can fall under *either* mindset.

Why is this important?

Simple. While E+R=O is the mindset that gets success principles working for you, E=O does the opposite. It switches the price tags!

Just as the thieves from earlier switched the price tags in the store to inflate the value of worthless items, E=O does the same thing. It gives top-dollar billing to what is beyond your control—events. And it does so while devaluing the one thing within your control—your mindset.

To make matters worse, E=O is sneaky. It breaks into your life when you're most vulnerable. When you're disappointed, frustrated, and frazzled because of tough times, that's when it's most likely to sneak in like a thief in the night and switch the price tags. But don't forget, it can do the same thing during good times. When you're confident and comfortable, if you let your guard down, it can also slip in and steal your Response-ABLE focus. Either way, E=O breaks in when you're most susceptible.

How can you tell if this is happening? What are the clues? Simply switch the price tags around on the success principles we just examined:

- Instead of taking small steps day in and day out to improve, start pinning your hopes on big breaks.
- Rather than working hard to make progress, make excuses about how things are unfair or that you're not talented enough.
- When things don't go your way, do what most people do—complain, blame, and belittle others.
- Instead of recognizing that struggles help you grow stronger, look for shortcuts.

In closing, both E+R=O and E=O serve as umbrellas under which all success principles fall. But only one mindset guarantees those principles work for you rather than against you, especially when you need them most. That's why E+R=O isn't just the most important mindset for success—it's the *only* mindset for success!

It's a Big Umbrella!

So…

Choose your mindset wisely.

Pick the one that gets success principles working for you instead of against you.

And once you do, don't let the price tags get switched.

★ ★ ★ ★ ★

> Now that we've established E+R=O as the unifying mindset that ties all success principles together, let's explore what fuels it in real life. It's time to talk about the determination and inner strength needed to turn intention into action.

Part 3

The Muscle Behind Grit

CHAPTER 6:

A WHOLE LOTTA ELVIS GOIN' ON

WHEN THE KING OF Rock 'n' Roll died in 1977, there were 48 professional Elvis Presley impersonators. By 1996, that number had grown to an astonishing 7,328. According to the Royal Statistical Society, if this growth rate had continued, by the year 2012, one in four people worldwide would have been Elvis impersonators.[1]

Can you imagine if this had come true? There would be a whole lot of people with bushy sideburns strutting around in beaded jumpsuits mumbling, "Thank you…Thank you very much."

A QUICK REVIEW

Before launching into the final section of this book, a quick review is in order. This review will accomplish two things. First, it will remind us of the main points covered so far. Second, it will set the table for what's next. This second point is noteworthy since what follows is the culmination of why E+R=O is the most powerful tool in our personal development toolbox.

As for the review, let's start with the overarching premise of the book:

- E+R=O stands for *Event + RESPONSE = Outcome*.
- E=O stands for *Event = Outcome*.
- These equations represent two of the predominant mindsets for how we live our lives.
- The purpose of this book, therefore, is to equip you to proactively choose an E+R=O mindset (rather than passively surrendering to E=O) because E+R=O is the only mindset for success.

With this as a backdrop, I began the book by asserting that E+R=O is a one-of-a-kind gift that changes a person from the inside out. Although it's not a big gift, it packs an incredible punch. The reason for this is the principle "BIG is Little and Little is BIG," which states that achieving anything significant in life requires small, positive actions day in and day out. However, to consistently take those actions, we must cultivate a mindset that enables us to overcome the resistance we will inevitably face. The mindset that helps us do this is E+R=O.

I also said that E+R=O is not a new gift. What I mean by this is that it's not something that comes from outside of us. It's a choice that originates from within each of us. That's why we all have the capacity to embrace an E+R=O mindset. However, most people don't make that choice. They either overlook E+R=O entirely or, at the very least, underutilize it. Therefore, to tap into this gift, we must first recognize the difference between E+R=O and E=O. Then, we must intentionally lean into E+R=O in our daily lives.

Lastly, I shared that E+R=O is not original with me. The concept has been around for a long time. While it goes by many different names, it is one of the most thoroughly researched theories in the field of personal development.

With these three descriptions as our underpinning, the book's first section demonstrated how E+R=O is "A Picture of Reality." That is to say, E+R=O is how the real world works (or at least how it works best). Specifically, we looked at the devastating effects of E=O and how it leads to learned helplessness and a victim mentality. By contrast, an E+R=O mindset leads to learned optimism and the ability to grow wiser, stronger, and more confident even in the midst of adversity.

In the second part of the book, we took a deep dive into how E+R=O is "The Foundation for Success." Chapter Three started by answering the question: "*What* is success?" I proposed that the best definition of success is not things like prestige, position, or prosperity. While none of these are bad, they do not make for a good definition of success. Consequently, my suggestion was to follow Stephen Covey's advice and begin with the end in mind. You do this by predetermining what matters most to you and then striving to live accordingly. This led to an explanation of how a personal purpose statement, based on your predetermined definition of success, can serve as a compass to guide you through life's journey.

After establishing a definition for success, Chapter Four explored "*how* E+R=O enables success" by outlining what it means to be Response-ABLE. Being Response-ABLE is different from being responsible. Whereas being responsible means doing what is expected of you (which, naturally, is good), being Response-ABLE takes it a step further. It means you take 100 percent ownership of your life and consciously choose your response, whether circumstances are good or bad. Put more bluntly, you refuse to allow feelings and circumstances to drive you. Instead, you live by predetermined values and priorities. I then introduced a tool called the 4 Fence Posts of Being Response-ABLE, which illustrates how E=O shrinks your life, while E+R=O expands it—no matter the events you encounter.

Finally, in Chapter Five, I explained "*why* E+R=O is the foundation for success." It's because E+R=O is the mindset that enables success principles to work for you, rather than against you. The word picture that best encapsulates this truth is that of an umbrella. E+R=O is the umbrella under which all success principles fall. To prove this point, we examined 10 success principles and revealed how E+R=O causes each of them to work in your favor.

THE REAL DEAL

As you can see, we have covered a lot. But frankly, we've only tackled the essentials—perhaps 25 percent of the actual value of E+R=O.

You might wonder how this is possible. How can we be more than halfway through the book and have only covered 25 percent of the value?

Well, remember, E+R=O is like a sapphire. It's multifaceted. That's why it took me almost 20 years to understand its most significant features. Since I learned the basics of E+R=O in bits and pieces over an extended period, I had a lot of disjointed information floating around in my head. I needed time to make sense of it all. This book is designed to shrink that learning curve for you. My hope is that you will understand the ins and outs of E+R=O immediately so you can put them into practice right away.

Moreover, as described in Chapter Four, to thoroughly understand and appreciate any significant truth, each of us must make our way through the Simplicity Bell Curve. As we complete this journey and arrive at the far side of the curve, we discover a new kind of simplicity—one that's deeper and more meaningful. It's better than the simplicity we had initially, which tends to be naive and immature. This new simplicity is more profound and well-informed. You can even say it is a truer understanding.

The Simplicity Bell Curve is also why the information we have examined thus far only represents 25 percent of E+R=O's value. Notice I did not say 25 percent of the *content*; I said 25 percent of the *value*. Please understand that most content on any given subject is foundational. That is to say, it is fundamental to understanding the topic. However, once a solid foundation is established, you can build upon it. And here's the key: *what is built upon that foundation is usually what is most valuable.*

Given this, the first two sections of this book have been the basics. They are the essentials for understanding E+R=O. Additionally, as the section titles suggest, they gave us "A Picture of Reality" and "The Foundation for Success." With these fundamentals as our building blocks, we can now proceed to the third part of the book and examine how E+R=O provides "The Muscle Behind Grit." This last feature is what makes E+R=O most valuable. Indeed, it is what moves us from being E+R=O impersonators to being the real deal. Just as Elvis impersonators can look like Elvis, sound like Elvis, and even move like Elvis, the truth is they are not Elvis. They only mimic what he did on the outside. They are not him on the inside.

Similarly, without understanding how E+R=O provides the muscle behind grit, we cannot advance beyond being a novice practitioner. We can talk about E+R=O. We can even apply E+R=O occasionally. But it won't be part of our DNA. We will be more impersonator than the real deal. More importantly, we will lack the mastery needed to become gritty, which is, by far, the most valuable aspect of E+R=O.

DEFINING GRIT

So, what is grit, and what can it do for you?

For the longest time, I was naive in my understanding of grit. I grasped the basic concept, but that was about it. I saw grit as solely the ability to push through pain when I didn't want to do something. In my mind, grit was nothing more than a grind-it-out mentality. Sort of a "Suck-It-Up-Buttercup" attitude at all times, no matter what.

Honestly, I believe most people have a similar view. This is also why most people aren't excited about developing grit. Who in their right mind wants to learn how to endure pain in order to do something they don't want to do?

But as Inigo Montoya said to Vizzini in *The Princess Bride*, "You keep using that word. I do not think it means what you think it means." That was certainly the case for me. Yet once I journeyed through the Simplicity Bell Curve and gained a truer understanding of how E+R=O is the muscle behind grit, I began to see grittiness in every successful person I met. Moreover, I became obsessed with developing grit myself.

Angela Duckworth is the author of the best-selling book *Grit*. Of all the research and books I have reviewed on grit,[2] she offers the best definition. But it's not just her definition that stands out; it's also the detailed explanation she gives prior to defining grit. That explanation is too lengthy to include here, so I'll only highlight a few key points. Still, I recommend picking up a copy of *Grit* for yourself. Just as Stephen Covey's *The 7 Habits of Highly Effective People* was one of the most influential books I read early in my career, Angela Duckworth's *Grit* has been one of the most impactful books I've read in the past decade. It's that good!

Duckworth identifies two key components of grit found in highly accomplished individuals. The first is "perseverance," and the second is "passion." After thoroughly explaining what she means by these two words, she summarizes her findings by writing:

> No matter the domain, the highly successful had a kind of ferocious determination that played out in two ways. First, these exemplars were unusually resilient and hardworking. Second, they knew in a very,

> *very deep way what it was they wanted. They not only had **determination**, they had **direction**. It was this combination of **passion** and **perseverance** that made high achievers special. In a word, they had grit (emphasis added).*³

Clearly, grit is not just a grind-it-out, "Suck-It-Up-Buttercup" mentality. True grit is much more! According to Duckworth, it is determination that is connected to direction. Perseverance that is married to passion.

Why is this combination so essential?

Unless you're a remarkably rare individual who can power through anything and everything, your ability to stick with something will eventually run out if you're missing either of these key ingredients. Think about it like this:

- Without passion, perseverance is pointless.
- Without perseverance, passion melts away in the face of adversity.

To summarize, using the four words Duckworth uses, grit is only possible when "perseverance" and "determination" are bolstered by "passion" and "direction."

THE MUSCLE BEHIND GRIT

Now that you have a basic understanding of grit, it's important to recognize that grit and talent are not the same—far from it.

While talent plays a role in success, it's never enough on its own to achieve your goals and dreams.

Why?

Because a person's natural ability or giftedness isn't the strongest predictor of success.

Grit is!

Although many people believe that talent is the most essential ingredient for success, research tells a different story. According to Duckworth and other experts, while talent matters, grit matters more. This explains why many talented individuals fail to reach their full potential—they often lack the perseverance to push through adversity. In contrast, those with less natural ability can achieve even greater success precisely because they develop grit. Their persistence enables them to steadily improve and eventually surpass their more naturally gifted peers. This is why I like to say, "Success is acquired, not inherited."

In summary, talent is necessary for success, but it's not enough to achieve your goals and dreams. To do that, you must also cultivate the ability to work hard and maintain your commitment over an extended period of time. It is this combination of talent and grit that enables an individual to become a high achiever.

Of course, adversity is inevitable in the pursuit of any meaningful goal. That's why you need the strength to get back up when life knocks you down. That is to say, you need the muscle to press on and keep going, no matter what events you face. And because life's greatest lessons are often learned in times of struggle, you also need the muscle to learn, grow, and develop through hardship.

Well…guess what?

The muscle behind grit[4]—the one that helps you get back up after you get knocked down and enables you to learn, grow, and develop during tough times—is none other than E+R=O!

Moreover, learning how E+R=O makes you grittier and then using that knowledge to accomplish your dreams and goals is, by far, the most valuable aspect of E+R=O. It is what infuses E+R=O into your DNA—moving you beyond being an impersonator and equipping you to become the real deal.

EXERCISING YOUR E+R=O MUSCLE

Again, you need both passion and direction, as well as perseverance and determination, to make all of this happen. They are the two sides of the grit coin. And, as you will see in the rest of this chapter and the next, E+R=O is the muscle behind each side. The more you strengthen your E+R=O muscle, the grittier you will become.

Having said that, it is crucial to realize that E+R=O exercises its muscle differently on each side of the grit coin. For instance, it is harder to decipher how E+R=O strengthens passion and direction than it is to understand how perseverance and determination are strengthened. The reason for this is simple. When we face adversity, it is easy to see E+R=O at work. That's because perseverance and determination are outwardly visible actions. By contrast, passion and direction are inward traits that are hard to observe.

The best way to explain these differences is with another analogy. While there are several types of muscles in the human body, the two primary types are cardiac and skeletal.

Cardiac muscles are the ones that keep the heart pumping blood throughout the circulatory system. These muscles perform their work in the background, meaning that most of the time, we are unaware of their activity. Nevertheless, these muscles are vital to life. According to Johns Hopkins Medicine, "Blood is the life-maintaining fluid that flows through blood vessels and carries nourishment, electrolytes, hormones, vitamins, antibodies, heat, and oxygen to the body."[5] Contrast these muscles to the skeletal muscles. Skeletal muscles control our voluntary nervous system, which means we use them when we decide to take any action. When we pick something up off the ground, go for a walk, or do any physical activity, we activate these muscles.

When it comes to both sides of the grit coin, the muscle behind the passion/direction side functions like a cardiac muscle, while the one behind the perseverance/determination side functions like a skeletal muscle.

Specifically, the muscle behind passion and direction, which is comparable to a cardiac muscle, pumps life-giving "blood" to grit. Similar to what electrolytes and vitamins do for the human body, this "blood" is filled with the nutrients grit needs to remain resilient when things get tough. Therefore, this muscle is not the behavior of grit. Instead, it is the *heartbeat* behind grit, always working in the background, pumping the nourishment it needs.

Conversely, the muscle behind perseverance and determination, which is comparable to a skeletal muscle, is associated with the action of grit. When people think of grit, this is what comes to mind. It is you consciously deciding that, no matter how hard something is or how long it takes, you will do it. This muscle is much easier to see because it is the outward expression of grit.

Whereas the previous muscle is the heartbeat behind grit, this one activates the *behavior* of grit.

THE HEARTBEAT MUSCLE BEHIND PASSION

Now that we have a basic understanding of E+R=O as the muscle behind grit, let's dive deeper into how each side of this muscle operates. We'll wrap up this chapter with a brief look at how E+R=O serves as the Heartbeat Muscle behind passion. Then, in Chapter Seven, we'll explore how E+R=O also functions as the Behavior Muscle behind perseverance.

There are at least three ways E+R=O strengthens the passion/direction side of grit. These three ways are purpose, goals, and a growth mindset.

PURPOSE

In Chapter Three, I explained how writing a personal purpose statement helps you stay focused on your predetermined definition of success. However, I didn't explain how to use your purpose statement. I said your purpose statement is like a compass, but I didn't share any practical tips.

In light of this, how do you use your purpose statement as a compass? Simple, take it out and look at it. That is to say, schedule regular times to review your purpose statement to make sure you're headed in the right direction. By reading it consistently, you align yourself with what is most important to you.

More specifically, if you create your purpose statement according to the guidelines laid out earlier, it's guaranteed to answer three of the biggest questions you can ask about life:

- The "One Thing" Question — If you boil life down to one truth or philosophy that makes life meaningful and valuable, what is it?
- The "Being" Question — How does this One Thing impact your Being? How does it shape who you are at your core?
- The "Doing" Question — How does this One Thing impact your Doing? How will it influence what you do with your life and how you do it?

Answering these questions is bound to create a weighty purpose statement. Having said that, creating such a statement may lead you to believe that reviewing it regularly will be burdensome because weighty statements are…well…weighty. But don't forget, the guidelines also showed you how to write a portable statement. This means that even a weighty purpose statement can be written concisely, allowing you to carry it with you.

The way I carry my purpose statement around with me is by routinely writing it out. At the start of most work days, I spend 10 to 15 minutes planning my day. Part of this routine includes determining what tasks I will focus on. But *before* I think about my tasks, I write down two other items that are more essential to my day:

- My purpose statement
- My three-to-five big goals for the year

Writing these two items first, before listing out my tasks, puts me in the right frame of mind. It centers me around what I have predetermined matters most. This allows me to live my day from the inside out, rather than from the outside in. It empowers me to lead my life according to my predetermined purpose and goals, rather than letting the events that happen to me dictate my life.

When I do this, I am being Response-ABLE and using the E+R=O Heartbeat Muscle to strengthen my passion. Remember, being Response-ABLE is different from being responsible. Being responsible is doing what is expected of you. Being Response-ABLE, however, means you purposefully look for ways to learn, grow, and develop no matter what events, good or bad, come your way. So, by writing out my purpose statement and goals at the start of the day, I take ownership of my day. I am choosing to be in charge. I am saying to myself, "This is what my life is about. No matter what happens today, I will live according to my purpose."

And don't miss this! The more you review your purpose and goals, the grittier you will become. This isn't because of some outward action you are taking (yes, you are writing out your purpose and goals, but that's it as far as actions go). No, it's because you're creating an E+R=O habit that serves you like a cardiac muscle. The more you focus on what you are passionate about (i.e., your purpose) and the direction you want to go (i.e., your goals), the more your "heart" pumps nourishment to your grittiness. You likely won't even realize this is happening because it all occurs in the background. But the next time you face adversity, you will be grittier because your perseverance and determination are now more closely aligned with your passion and direction.

How cool is that?!

GOALS

A second way the E+R=O Heartbeat Muscle strengthens your passion and direction is through goals. I just mentioned that I write down my top three to five annual goals every day. While I could share a lot more about goals, that's not the purpose of this book. If you want to dive deeper into setting and achieving goals, you can receive free access to a video coaching program I produced, titled "Goal Getting." Just visit **KENTJULIAN.COM/RESPONSEBOOK** for more information.

Still, there is one strategy I'd like to share, as it's an effective tool for bolstering your passion. The idea comes from Dan Sullivan, the president of Strategic Coach®. It's a simple question he asks all his clients. The question is this: "If we were having this discussion three years from today, and you were looking back over those three years, what has to have happened in your life, both personally and professionally, for you to feel happy with your progress?"[6]

What I love about this question is that it not only helps you set goals that you are passionate about, but it also ensures those goals are aligned with the direction you want to go. Here's how…

First, if you can look back on your life three years from now and feel happy with your progress, it will likely be because you have been pursuing goals you are passionate about achieving. Otherwise, you wouldn't be satisfied.

Second, you are most likely passionate about these goals because they are connected to the direction you want to go. Namely, they are connected to your life's purpose.

In summary, using Dan Sullivan's question to help you set goals provides "nourishment" to your goals by connecting them to the passion and direction you are pursuing. This means when adversity strikes (and it will strike), your Heartbeat Muscle will already be pumping nutrients through your "bloodstream." These nutrients will be working behind the scenes to give you the strength to push through with your goals when things get tough.

GROWTH MINDSET

One final way the E+R=O Heartbeat Muscle strengthens your passion is through a growth mindset, which I believe is the most powerful aspect of the Heartbeat Muscle.

If you recall the research I shared earlier from Martin Seligman regarding learned helplessness versus learned optimism, the phrases "fixed mindset" and "growth mindset" might sound similar. That's because they are. In this case, learned helplessness and a fixed mindset go together, while learned optimism and a growth mindset do the same. Once again, to use an analogy, think of each pair as teammates. In fact, think of them as professional wrestling tag teams—one made up of the good guys, the other of the villains.

As a quick reminder, learned helplessness is a condition that causes individuals to perceive events deterministically. Therefore, when something negative happens, they view it as permanent and pervasive. As a result, they feel defeated even when the littlest thing goes wrong. This is why these people give up more easily and fall into depression more often.

By contrast, learned optimism causes people to view bad events as temporary. This helps them overcome adversity and become more resilient.

Now, the difference between a fixed mindset and a growth mindset is similar, but not exactly the same. According to Carol Dweck, author of the book *Mindset*, if you have a fixed mindset, you believe people's traits and abilities are set in stone. Each individual has "a *certain* amount of intelligence, a *certain* personality, and a *certain* moral character" (emphasis added).[7] These certainties are the "hand you are dealt and have to live with."[8] The implication is that there's little, if anything, you can do to change them.

Alternatively, a growth mindset sees "the hand you are dealt as just the starting point for development…your basic qualities are things you can cultivate through your efforts, your strategies, and help from others. Although people may differ in every which way—in their initial talents and aptitudes, interests, or temperaments—everyone can change and grow through application and experience."[9]

Can you see how learned helplessness and a fixed mindset go hand in hand, while learned optimism and a growth mindset likewise do? Each pair feeds off of one another and ends up working together. And in case you're wondering, the first pair is the villainous tag team, while the second is the good guys. To clarify, learned helplessness and a fixed mindset are the bad guys who work together to shrink your life, while learned optimism and a growth mindset are the good guys who work together to expand it.

Furthermore, did you notice that the partners for each tag team play a similar role to one of the partners on the other tag team? For example, despite learned helplessness being the villain and learned optimism being the good guy, both focus on the *events* that happen to us. Learned helplessness believes events, especially negative ones, are permanent and will automatically undermine that person's life. On the other hand, learned optimism believes events are temporary and can be overcome.

By comparison, a fixed mindset and a growth mindset focus on a person's *response* rather than the event. A fixed mindset (i.e., the villain) believes there is nothing people can do to change the hand they are dealt in life. Alternatively, a growth mindset (i.e., the good guy) believes there is a lot people can do to improve their hand.

All of this is to say, whether you are aware of it or not, one of these two tag teams is constantly at work in the background of your life. For instance, if you allow learned helplessness and a fixed mindset to take over, your mind will be fueled by thoughts like:

- *There is nothing I can do.*
- *That's just the way I am.*
- *These kinds of things always happen to me.*
- *I should give up.*

Do you see how nefarious this tag team is? All they want to do is pin you to the mat by using negative events to ruin your life. That's why you must fight them at every turn!

The other tag team—learned optimism and a growth mindset—does the opposite. They don't ignore or deny events, but they aren't entirely focused on them either. Instead, they look for the best way to respond. Once again, while you might be unaware of how this duo works in the background, they are still there, filling your mind with thoughts like:

- *I can overcome this adversity.*
- *My attitude and effort count.*

- *I can choose a different approach.*
- *When I fall, I can get back up.*

This is why they are the good guys. They want you to learn, grow, and get better through every challenge you face. So be sure to listen to them—they are on your side!

REAL DEAL DNA

From cardiac and skeletal muscles to tag-team wrestlers, this chapter has featured several analogies. But let's revisit the one I used to kick things off. Just as Elvis impersonators are not Elvis, E+R=O novices are not the real deal either. They might be able to talk about E+R=O and occasionally put it into practice, but it isn't who they are on the inside.

To become the real deal—to have E+R=O ingrained into your DNA—you must travel through the Simplicity Bell Curve to gain a deeper, more meaningful understanding. It's not enough to see this mindset as simply "A Picture of Reality" and "The Foundation for Success." Yes, these are fundamental truths, but they're meant to be built upon. They lay the groundwork for unlocking the greatest value of E+R=O.

What is the greatest value?

It is the realization that E+R=O is "The Muscle Behind Grit."

So far, we have explored one way E+R=O acts as the muscle behind grit—working behind the scenes as a Heartbeat Muscle, pumping nourishment to the passion/direction side of grit. We needed to start here because, as Angela Duckworth states, "Grit isn't *just* working incredibly hard. That's only part of it....Grit is about working on something you care about so much that you're willing to stay loyal to it."[10] Doing the three things we talked about in this chapter—regularly reviewing your purpose, pursuing goals that make you come alive, and nourishing a growth mindset—are practices that will help you stay loyal to what you care about.

However, for grit to be truly gritty, we must add perseverance and determination to the mix. To quote Duckworth again, "Considering all the studies showing that gritty people typically stick with their commitment longer than others, it seemed like the major advantage of grit was, simply, more time on task."[11]

★ ★ ★ ★ ★

> "More time on task"—that is the focus of the upcoming chapter. It is also where you will see, more vividly than anywhere else, why E+R=O is the most valuable tool in your personal-development toolbox.

CHAPTER 7:

MUSCLE UP (WITHOUT STEROIDS)

YEARS AGO, WHEN TALK shows were a novelty on television, the host of a popular show interviewed a bodybuilder. Bodybuilding was also relatively new, so the host asked his guest a simple question: "Why do you develop those particular muscles?"

With that, the bodybuilder stood up…stepped forward…and launched into an impressive routine of flexes. The audience erupted into applause. Once he finished, the bodybuilder sat down, waiting for the next question.

The host didn't miss a beat.

"That's nice, but I'm still unclear. What do you use all those muscles for?"

Once again, the man stepped forward and posed. He flexed from top to bottom—chest, biceps, quads, and calves.

Not to be deterred, the host asked one last time, "But what do you *use* those muscles for?"

The bodybuilder was bewildered. He couldn't answer the question. Evidently, the only reason he worked out was to strike poses and flex his muscles in all their glory.[1]

DON'T BE A POSER

In the previous chapter, I explained how E+R=O is the muscle behind grit and why this is, by far, the most valuable aspect of E+R=O.

Additionally, I said that E+R=O exercises this muscle in two ways. The first, as described in the previous chapter, is as a Heartbeat Muscle. Just as cardiac muscles work behind the scenes to pump blood through our physical body, E+R=O works in the background to nourish and sustain the passion and direction side of grit.

The second way E+R=O channels its strength is as a Behavior Muscle. In this chapter, you'll learn how E+R=O uses this muscle to build resilience and boost determination. According to Angela Duckworth, these qualities are key to unlocking the greatest benefit of grit, which is "more time on task."

More time on task—what exactly does that mean?

Obviously, it means dedicating more time to tasks, but it goes deeper than that. It is endurance over the long haul. It is staying committed to something even when that something is difficult. It is tenacity in both good times and challenging times. In a word, more time on task is *stick-to-it-tiveness*.

How important is stick-to-it-tiveness?

Without it, grit is like a clueless bodybuilder who doesn't know why he develops his muscles. Sure, he can strike poses, but for what purpose? Only to look good? No, for grit to be gritty, it must behave like grit. It must have stamina. It must endure. And it must use these qualities to dedicate more time to tasks.

Furthermore, stick-to-it-tiveness is the main advantage of cultivating grit. As we discovered in the previous chapter, resilience and determination, more than raw talent or aptitude, are what drive high achievement and success. Again, as Duckworth said in her famous TED Talk, "One characteristic emerged [from all our research] as a significant predictor of success. It wasn't social intelligence. It wasn't good looks, physical health, and it wasn't IQ. It was grit."[2]

Bottom line: Grit proves one thing above all else—stick-to-it-tiveness matters! So, how do you build that kind of perseverance into your daily life? Let's walk through what it takes to strengthen grit's Behavior Muscle.

THE BEHAVIOR MUSCLE BEHIND PERSEVERANCE

To better understand how to grow your resolve and determination, this chapter examines seven strategies for strengthening the E+R=O Behavior Muscle behind grit. As you implement these strategies, your ability to spend more time on tasks, particularly those related to your passions, will improve. However, before moving forward, we should consider a few fundamental truths about high achievement and success.

First, there is no magic pill. You probably noticed the word "steroids" in the chapter title. I used it intentionally because many people try to solve their problems with quick fixes or shortcuts. However, when it comes to stick-to-it-tiveness, there are no quick fixes. And shortcuts only lead to fake muscles and empty poses. To grow grit, you must put in the work.

Second, don't forget "BIG Is Little and Little Is BIG." This success principle is emphasized throughout the book for good reason. Taking the right little actions, day in and day out, is what eventually leads to big results. So, while talent and skill play a role in achievement, persistence is indispensable. And, as you will see, the following seven strategies are all small actions you can take that lead to big successes.

Third, grit grows from the inside out. The previous chapter demonstrated how grit fades without passion and direction. That's because when grit is disconnected from passion, it doesn't know what to use its muscles for. In contrast, your determination grows stronger when you are passionate about something. The reason for this is simple—inward passion fuels outward perseverance. That's why grit grows from the inside out.

THE SEVEN EXERCISES

With these three realities as our basic footing for high achievement and success, we can now explore the seven exercises to strengthen your E+R=O Behavior Muscle. Building this muscle will increase your resilience and determination, enabling you to pursue your goals and dreams more effectively, especially when the going gets tough.

1. KEEP YOUR COMMITMENTS

The following seven strategies are presented in no particular order—except for this one. This strategy is first because it's the most crucial for building the Behavior Muscle behind grit. It also serves as the cornerstone for all the other strategies.

Every time you make a commitment and follow through on it—whether it's to yourself or someone else—you get stronger. For instance, you become stronger internally whenever you follow through on commitments to yourself. Likewise, your relationships grow stronger when you follow through with commitments made to others.

Alternatively, the fastest way to become a poser is to break your word. When you break your word with someone else, that person is less likely to trust you next time. Similarly, when you break a promise to yourself, you lose a bit of inner integrity, and it becomes easier to break personal promises in the future.

In light of this, how can you use E+R=O to strengthen your ability to keep commitments? Here are four ideas:

First, remember "BIG Is Little and Little Is BIG." Don't go overboard making extravagant promises to yourself or others. Concentrate on doing a few things and doing them well.

Second, watch your mouth. Since it's uncomfortable to disappoint others, we sometimes say "yes" to things we don't intend to do. However, the truth is that whether you say "yes" or "no," you will feel uncomfortable at some point. If you say "yes" to a commitment you don't plan to keep just to avoid feeling uncomfortable, you will eventually experience the discomfort of being untrustworthy. Meanwhile, if you choose not to commit to something, you might feel uncomfortable in the moment, but you avoid the discomfort of breaking your word later on. Personally, I'd rather not commit to something and feel uncomfortable in the moment than deal with the distress of breaking my promise later on. (By the way, it took me a long time to learn this lesson.)

Third, remember that "Habits MAKE You or BREAK You." Do you recall what Brian Tracy said about this success principle? "Good habits are hard to form, but easy to live with. Bad habits…are easy to form, but hard to live with." This is especially true when it comes to keeping commitments. For example, in order to follow through on a promise, you have to remember the promise, establish a plan for keeping the promise, and then do the work of fulfilling the promise. Clearly, this is an excellent habit. But don't kid yourself; it isn't easy to form. It requires conscientious choices and ongoing effort. Yet once you develop this habit, it will make your life easier. (To build stronger habits, check out this two-page guide: "10 Daily Habits of Highly Successful People." Visit KENTJULIAN.COM/RESPONSEBOOK to get this resource.)

Finally, ask for forgiveness. No one is perfect. Despite your best intentions, you will occasionally fail to keep your commitments. When this happens, don't just apologize. Ask for forgiveness. There is something powerful about going beyond simply saying you're sorry (i.e., an apology) to humbly asking someone to do something for you that you don't deserve (i.e., forgiveness). It's the ultimate way of taking responsibility for your mistake.

Furthermore, this step will mature you, regardless of whether the other person forgives you or not.

As a side note, most people forgive me if I sincerely ask for forgiveness. Even more, I've found that not only is their trust in me restored, but it's often strengthened. I'm not sure why this is, but I believe it's because they realize I'm taking ownership of my life, even the ugly side.

2. ALREADY, NOT YET STATEMENTS

This strategy builds upon the previous one. Therefore, if you struggle keeping promises and commitments—especially those that matter most to you—this will help.

I used to be a fan of personal affirmation statements. I even wrote a short workbook titled *Affirm Yourself*. However, I am no longer a fan.

My initial enthusiasm came from taking the word "affirmation" at face value. A classic definition of an affirmation is "the assertion of something true." For instance, in his book *The Five Love Languages*, Gary Chapman teaches "Words of Affirmation" as one of the five love languages. When people verbally share their admiration and appreciation for someone, they are practicing this love language. But don't overlook this fact—the verbal message shared *must be true*. Otherwise, the person is using flattery rather than being affirming, and that's not an act of love; it's a lie.

When I first heard that writing down and repeating affirmations was a personal-development strategy, I naively believed that was all it was—creating *factual* statements I could repeat to myself that would help me build something positive into my life or change something negative. But the deeper I looked into the practice, the more I realized how misleading it actually is. In fact, most teachings about affirmations commit a kind of linguistic theft—they co-opt the word and distort its meaning. As a result, personal affirmations have little to do with truth. Instead, they involve repeating made-up statements—or outright fantasies—with the blind hope that saying them enough times will somehow make them real. It's not about clarity or honesty; it's wishful thinking dressed up as self-help.

To be clear, there are two primary reasons I am no longer a fan of affirmations. The first is relatively harmless. The second, not so much.

The first reason I am not a fan is because many of the affirmations being taught today are just silly. No kidding, here are actual affirmation statements I've heard in training:

- "Working toward my goals is constantly easy for me."
- "Super cool things are coming my way. Guaranteed!"
- "I am a money magnet. Money automatically flows into my bank account."

Sorry, but phrases like these are meaningless and do more harm than good. Why? Because repeating fictional statements and pretending they can magically come true is silly at best and unrealistic at worst.

First of all, none of these statements is based on reality. Accomplishing worthwhile goals is rarely easy. No one can guarantee super cool things come their way. And money automatically flowing into your bank account? I want to meet that person.

Second, each statement focuses on events outside of your

control. You cannot control how easily you achieve your goals. You cannot guarantee super cool things come your way. And you cannot cause money to automatically flow into your bank account.

Finally, while these statements sound positive, each sets you up for disappointment. What happens if goals aren't easy to achieve? Or if super cool things don't come your way? Or if the only direction money flows is *out* of your bank account? Yikes!

But the second reason I am not a fan of affirmation statements is more serious. As hinted at a few paragraphs ago, many people view affirmations as declarations that have the power to bring things into existence. Put more bluntly, they believe affirmations can supernaturally alter reality or even create something out of nothing. This is why they are often referred to as "manifestations."

Let's be clear—our words are powerful. They can inspire us, shape our thinking, and motivate us to action. However, they do not have the power to alter reality or bring something into existence. So, while speaking positive truths to yourself is a good practice, believing affirmations can magically make something happen is wishful thinking. And if that isn't enough, when people buy into the "abracadabra" illusion that affirmations can somehow alter reality, they rob themselves of acquiring life skills such as critical thinking, hard work, and persistence. Why is this harmful? Because these are the life skills needed to strengthen the E+R=O Behavior Muscle behind grit.

Now, before throwing rotten tomatoes at me (or worse, canned tomatoes), hear me out. There is a way to write realistic, positive, *truthful* statements that affirm the one thing that is 100 percent within your control—your response. I call these *Already, Not Yet* statements.

What is an Already, Not Yet statement? It is a:

- Powerful, positive statement about your personhood…
- That you *already* believe and want to be true about your life…
- But, if you are honest, it is *not yet* a reality.

In other words, Already, Not Yet statements are truthful, affirming statements that you repeat to yourself in order to shape who you are striving to be in the present and who you want to become in the future. They differ from the affirmations I just described in two ways. First, they focus on inward traits rather than outward events. Why is this essential? Because you can cultivate inward character traits, but as repeated throughout this book, you are not in control of outward events.

Second, while Already, Not Yet statements include a description of the outcome you hope to achieve, that is not their primary focus. Their main priority is on who you desire to become. Do you hope to achieve the outcome described in your statement? Of course. But again, that's not the primary emphasis. The emphasis is on *you* and *your character*.

Here's an example of an Already, Not Yet statement that helped me make a positive change in my life. After a decade of marriage, Kathy and I faced a tough season. One of the problems on my end was that I often prioritized my career ahead of my wife and kids. To be clear, I *already* loved Kathy more than any other person on earth. And our three children were the next three people I loved the most. I also *already* wanted to put them first and show them how important they were to me. However, the uncomfortable truth is I was *not yet* living this consistently. When push came to shove, my career and the dreams I had for the business I wanted to build often took priority.

One day, while journaling, I wrote the following statement:

> I daily choose to live my life
> in such a way that Kathy and our kids
> can look at me and say with pride,
> "That's my husband," and 'That's my dad."

This was a breakthrough moment for me. It provided me with an Already, Not Yet statement that achieved the two things I mentioned. First, it forced me to think deeply about the inward traits I needed to work on to be a better husband and dad. This was something within my power to achieve. Second, it included the hopeful outcome of my wife and kids being proud of me. That wasn't the primary emphasis of the statement, as I couldn't guarantee it would happen. Nevertheless, if I consistently took steps to become a better husband and father, that outcome would likely occur.

As a side note, I've repeated this phrase to myself for over twenty years, and I can honestly say that I have become a better husband and father as a result. I can also say that the outcome I hoped for has come true as well. I am both fortunate and grateful.

3. TALK BACK TO E=O

When life is smooth sailing, our need for resilience and determination is low. However, when life gets stormy...that's a different story.

Yet here's the problem: Most people's brains (including mine) are hardwired to believe E=O. This means when bad events happen, we naturally default to E=O thinking.

So, what's a person to do?

Talk back to your E=O thinking!

There are several ways to talk back to E=O, but the best I've found is to ask yourself Response-ABLE questions. For example, when bad events happen, instead of making statements like "this sort of thing always happens to me" (i.e., learned helplessness) or "there is nothing I can do" (i.e., fixed mindset), ask Response-ABLE questions such as:

- "What can I do?"
- "What responses are within my control?"
- "What does this make possible?"

That last question is my favorite. It quickly moves me away from focusing exclusively on events and toward thinking about possibilities.

As you recall from Chapter Five, I learned to ask this question from my friend and mentor, Dan Miller. The question wasn't original to Dan, but he asked it whenever he faced challenges, including when he lost his business and spent 12 years recovering financially. Let that sink in. In his early 40s, Dan was devastated by a business failure, and he didn't get back to zero until his mid-50s. Yet, instead of wallowing in misery, Dan slowly dug himself out of that massive hole and eventually built a highly successful business. He did it by constantly asking himself, "What does this make possible?"

To be clear, Dan wasn't living in a fantasy during those days. He knew what he was up against. But he also knew the only way out was to concentrate on what was within his control. So, rather than seeing his problems as just problematic, he saw them as "opportunities looking for solutions" (another one of Dan's favorite sayings). I never met anyone who talked back to E=O the way he did, and I am thankful he passed that wisdom along to me.

4. STEP INTO E=O (BUT ONLY FOR A MOMENT)

When we face adversity, especially like the one Dan faced, we kid ourselves if we believe we can immediately switch gears and start thinking E+R=O. Business failures, serious illnesses, the death of a loved one, betrayal, losing a job—these crises can turn our world upside down.

Therefore, even though it's important to talk back to E=O thinking, don't expect to do so right away. We are not robots. We need time to process, feel our emotions, and vent. The key, of course, is not to get stuck there.

Given this, go ahead and get things off your chest. Complain about unfair treatment. Talk about what went wrong. But once you get your frustrations out, move on to asking Response-ABLE questions. Doing so will help you move forward faster. And, as an added benefit, it will also help you process your feelings more effectively.

5. PROACTIVELY GROW YOUR FENCE POSTS

Remember our definition of being Response-ABLE? It's not just doing what is expected of you; it's going a step further. It's taking 100 percent ownership of *all* your responses, whether the events you face are good or bad. It also means you are driven by values and priorities rather than feelings and circumstances.

To illustrate this, I introduced the 4 Fence Posts of Being Response-ABLE. As you recall, each fence post represents a personal area over which we have 100 percent ownership. This means each of us is entirely in charge of our:

- Attitude
- Associations (both who we associate with and what content we allow into our lives)
- Articulation (the words we say to others and ourselves)
- Actions

These fence posts illustrate how our life shrinks when we refuse to be Response-ABLE. They also show how our life expands once we take charge of our attitude, associations, articulation, and actions.

Having reminded you of this, one thing I didn't say in Chapter Four is that the language I used was more *defensive* than offensive. That is to say, it was more reactive than proactive. This is because that chapter's focus was on events that have already happened or were still unfolding.

However, since reading that chapter, we've progressed through the Simplicity Bell Curve, so our understanding of

E+R=O should be more robust. This progress means we are now ready to examine the *offensive* dimensions of the 4 Fence Posts. Specifically, here's how you can use each Fence Post to prepare for future events.

Attitude — Here are three quick ways to proactively improve your attitude. All of these should be self-explanatory. First, read and listen to uplifting content to better prepare yourself for the future. Second, at the start of each day, write down at least three things you are thankful for—this simple practice will put you in a grateful frame of mind. Third, remember that having a good attitude doesn't mean you're always excited or giddy. When you face challenging times, you don't have to pretend to be happy about them. That's not a positive attitude—that's just fake. A good attitude means being gritty. It's saying, "No matter how hard this is or how long it takes, I'm going to figure things out." That's a truly positive attitude.

Associations — Author and speaker Jim Rohn is credited with saying, "You are the average of the five people you spend the most time with." In light of this, be selective about who you allow to speak into your life. Also, make wise choices about the content that crosses your eyes and enters your ears.

Articulation — Years ago, I heard a saying that has shaped my leadership ever since. The saying is, "Always build up, never tear down." This does not mean that I'm afraid to stand up for the truth or say tough things. However, it does mean I don't intentionally try to tear someone down when a hard conversation is necessary. Instead, I speak as gently as possible while still being candid. My goal is to proactively build the other person up by speaking the truth graciously, even when strong or intense words are required.

This is a hard skill to develop, and I'm far from perfect at it, but it's something I continue to work on.

Actions — There are many ways to apply E+R=O to become more Response-ABLE in your actions, but perhaps the most effective is to learn from your mistakes and those of others. As the saying goes, "Never waste a good mistake." Blunders and missteps, especially painful ones, open our eyes to new learning. Moreover, these lessons become deeply ingrained in our psyche because no one in their right mind wants to repeat the same failures. In short, learning from mistakes is one of the most proactive paths to wisdom, and it's a fantastic way to prepare for future challenges.

6. GO BACK TO SCHOOL

Another great way to become grittier is to "go back to school" and learn from other gritty people. Does that mean you have to buy a book bag and jump back into the classroom? Certainly not. You can learn about grit by reading biographies, listening to podcast interviews, and observing how gritty people behave.

A great place to begin this education is with your heroes. As you know, I loved basketball in middle and high school. Two of my basketball heroes are Mark Price and Larry Bird. As a lifelong Georgia Tech fan, I watched Mark Price lead the Yellow Jackets out of obscurity to become a dominant force in college basketball. Larry Bird did the same for the Boston Celtics in the NBA. If you're not a basketball fan, it might surprise you that both these players lacked the physical attributes of other great players. Speed. Leaping ability. Neither possessed these qualities in abundance.

What exactly did they have?

GRIT. Loads and loads of grit!

Grit was front and center whenever I watched them play. But I also heard about their grit in interviews with coaches and players. They would say things like, "He doesn't have loads of natural talent (*event*), but he makes up for it with his work ethic (*response*). He is the first to show up for practice and the last to leave the court. All that hard work has turned him into one of the elite players in the game, and his example elevates the rest of the team (*outcome*)." What a vivid illustration of how growing your E+R=O Behavior Muscle—and developing grit—can make a significant difference in your performance.

Another place to get this kind of schooling is through biographies. I've learned many E+R=O lessons from biographies and documentaries. Here's a sampling of the historical figures who have influenced my life:

- United States Presidents like John Adams, Abraham Lincoln, and Teddy Roosevelt.
- Olympians like Wilma Rudolph, Jesse Owens, and Katie Ledecky.
- People who have overcome physical challenges, such as Helen Keller and Bethany Hamilton.
- Heroes who fought slavery and racism, including Frederick Douglass, William Wilberforce, and Booker T. Washington.
- Inventors like the Wright Brothers.
- Prisoners of war such as Viktor Frankl and Lee Ellis.
- Business leaders like Mary Kay Ashe and Truett Cathy.

One of my favorite biographical heroes is Dr. Ben Carson. Talk about determination and perseverance! He is a shining example of how to turn your greatest adversities into your greatest advantages. If you haven't read his autobiography *Gifted Hands*, I highly recommend it.

Often, the best education is in your own backyard. I already introduced you to Dan Miller. I learned a lot about E+R=O and grit from Dan.

Another friend I've learned a lot from is Andy Perkins. After nearly two decades of knowing him, I'm still blown away by his story.

As a child, Andy loved his family, but he never felt like he belonged. He struggled throughout school, so at age 20, he joined the Army and spent the next 10 years stationed all over the world.

Toward the end of those 10 years, Andy decided to take up running. What made this feat extraordinary was that he was a two-pack-a-day smoker at the time. Nevertheless, once he committed to running marathons, he quit smoking within a few years and began training 10 miles a day in hot, humid conditions. This dedication ultimately led to race invitations worldwide and several championships.

After retiring from the Army, Andy settled in Texas, and he and his beautiful bride had six children. He worked in printing for the next 15 years and eventually founded his own company. During that time, Andy decided to take a trip to Liberia. He explains it by saying, "I wanted to see what a country in civil war was like." But later, to his surprise, he said, "I fell in love with the Liberian people on that trip." Wanting to do something to help his new friends, Andy used his vacation days every year to return to Liberia and teach people how to start small businesses.

In January 2005, Andy was diagnosed with Stage IV cancer. He was told to get his affairs in order because, according to the doctor, "You have very little time left." But after surgery and a year of chemo, he was miraculously cancer-free and has remained so for almost 20 years. Even more amazing is that he returned to Liberia two months after being declared in remission.

What happened next changed Andy forever. It's also when his E+R=O Behavior Muscle went into overdrive. You see, Andy has ADD (i.e., Attention Deficit Disorder). As he says, "I am off the chart! I test over 90 on a scale of 100." As a result, Andy never stuck with anything in the past. "After a few years of doing something, I get bored. I would zone out when I reached a rudimentary level of competence." However, in February 2006, all of that changed, and he has been fully engaged in serving the Liberian people ever since.

What happened in February 2006?

Andy went to Liberia for a month to figure out what to do with his new lease on life. While there, he observed a four-year-old girl "willingly" being sexually abused for a handful of rice. He ran down the alley to stop what was happening, but as the abuser ran off, instead of being angry with him, the little girl became angry *with Andy*. Why? Because Andy had just cost her the only food she would get that day, perhaps even for several days. This broke Andy's heart. He says, "I instantly had a new set of eyes. For the first time, I saw hundreds of hungry, malnourished children all around the city of Buchanan. I had traveled there every year for seven years and never saw it before. I was devastated, and I had to take action. The problem was, I had no skills. I didn't have a clue about what it takes to feed hungry children or start a non-profit organization. But that didn't matter because I *had* to do something!"

So, in May 2008, Andy stepped into his new calling and opened a feeding center. He immediately had 150 malnourished children in his program, and despite not knowing how to run this venture, he was committed to feeding every child.

During the first eight months, 18 children died from malaria, typhoid, cholera, and dysentery. However, during those dark days, he learned what needed to be done and how to accomplish it. And now, almost 20 years later, BESTWA—the non-profit Andy founded—provides food, medical care, and clothing for over 1,000 children each day. They also offer education and medical services to hundreds of people. Case in point: In 2024, BESTWA provided scholarships and schooling for 336 elementary school students, 19 secondary school students, and four university students. They also supplied medical equipment, medicine, and clean birth kits to hospitals, clinics, and individual mothers. Finally, they performed 51 life-saving surgeries at their birthing clinics for mothers facing death during childbirth. This is just a sampling of what BESTWA accomplishes annually.[3]

There is still one more E+R=O insight to share about Andy. Just when I thought his life couldn't be more astonishing, on January 23, 2020, at the age of 70, Andy learned that he isn't Andrew James Perkins. He is actually Phillip Keith Robinson and was accidentally switched at birth with another baby. The details of this story are too numerous to share here, but if you want to read more, check out the *New York Post* article titled, "I Always Looked Different Than the Rest of My Family—Turns Out I Was Switched at Birth."[4]

I'm sure you can imagine how stunned I was when Andy texted me to share this latest twist in his life. I immediately called to check on him, and when I asked what he thought about this unbelievable turn of events, Andy responded in true E+R=O fashion. "Kent, I can't change anything *(event)*, and honestly, I wouldn't if I could *(response)*. I've lived an unbelievable life. And now, when some people have no family, I have two *(outcome)*!"

Being friends with Andy is an incredible gift. For one, he is older than I am, so I've gained a lot from his wisdom over the years. But two, our friendship has given me a front-row seat to watch someone I love and respect flex both sides of his E+R=O muscle. When I say "flex," I don't mean like a bodybuilder. Andy isn't a poser; he's the real deal. He has shown me firsthand the remarkable difference a person can make in the world when passion is combined with perseverance.

7. REVERSE INTERVIEW

This last strategy is probably my favorite. I've gained more insight and wisdom from *Reverse Interviewing* than just about anything else.

What is Reverse Interviewing?

It's similar to finding heroes in biographies and documentaries, but it's more personal and powerful. Here's how it works…

Early in my career, I was fortunate to meet several highly successful people in my field. They were sharp, well spoken, and each held to a high standard of excellence. Since I looked up to them and wanted to find out what they had done to achieve success, I asked each person to join me individually for breakfast or lunch. I don't remember whether this idea originated from someone else or if I thought of it myself, but I do recall coming up with the phrase "Reverse Interview." I called it this because I was "interviewing" them, even though they were my superiors.

Every single person accepted my offer, and I learned so much from those first few Reverse Interviews that it started a trend with me. As I shared earlier, when Kathy and I were engaged, I wanted to learn how to be the best husband I could be. So, I conducted Reverse Interviews with men who had great marriages. I took the same approach when I became a new father. And through the years, each time I wanted to learn something new—how to purchase a house, how to invest money wisely, how to interview for a new position, how to write a book, how to start a business, how to become a professional speaker—I found people to Reverse Interview.

After hundreds of breakfasts and lunches, I've learned a lot about conducting Reverse Interviews. Here are a few helpful guidelines:

Don't be afraid to ask. While randomly asking someone to breakfast or lunch may feel awkward the first few times you do it, most people will be honored that you asked them once you explain your reasoning.

Pick up the check. This is extremely important! I have Reverse Interviewed hundreds of people, many of whom are much wealthier than I am. Several have offered to pick up the check, but I've never let them. Why? Because they're doing *me* a service. They're sharing valuable insight with me, so it's only right (and professional) that I pay for their meal. By the way, if you can't afford to pick up the check for a meal (I've been there), ask the person out for coffee. But no matter what, YOU PAY.

Don't waste time. When meeting for a Reverse Interview, after a few minutes of pleasantries, say something like, "Thank you for meeting with me. I respect your time, so I'd like to start asking you questions. I know there is much I can learn from you." Then, pull out a legal pad or notebook with all your questions written down and fire away. As a side note, I don't write my questions on a mobile device or tablet because I want the interviewee to see my notes and realize how serious I am about our conversation. I cannot begin to tell you how many people have said they're impressed to see all the questions I've prepared and that I'm taking notes.

Ask for advice. As you approach the end of the Reverse Interview, say something like, "As you can see from my notes, I have eight to 10 additional questions, but since we only have 15 minutes left, I'd like to wrap up with a different kind of question. I'm still new to learning about this subject, which means I don't know what I don't know. Therefore, what advice do you have for me that I haven't asked about?" This is my favorite question because it uncovers insights and secrets to success I'm clueless about—things I wouldn't even have thought to ask.

End the meeting on time. If you're meeting for lunch from 12:30 to 1:30 PM, wrap things up by 1:30 PM (unless the other person offers to extend the meeting).

Send a handwritten thank-you note afterwards. This is a common courtesy that demonstrates respect and professionalism.

Conducting Reverse Interviews is like adding rocket fuel to your learning, growth, and development. I cannot think of another strategy that has paid bigger dividends to my personal and professional progress than sitting across the table from accomplished people and learning from their life lessons. I guarantee it will do the same for you.

FULL BODY WORKOUT

All seven exercises we just reviewed can help you build your E+R=O Behavior Muscle. But unlike the bodybuilder mentioned at the start of the chapter, you won't just be flexing—you'll be equipped to take real action in pursuit of your goals and dreams by investing more time on task.

How does this happen?

Let me break it down, both technically and simply.

Technically, every time you use one of these strategies, you are working your E+R=O Behavior Muscle in a slightly different way. Therefore, the more consistently you practice each strategy, the more complete your "full-body workout" becomes. Over time, this builds grit and stick-to-it-tiveness, helping E+R=O become part of your DNA.

But here's the simple answer (and the one you are more likely to remember): The more you train your response muscle, the more naturally E+R=O becomes your way of life.

That's simple…and powerful!

✯ ✯ ✯ ✯ ✯

> Congratulations! You've now got the mindset.
>
> But before we close out the book, let's take one final step—literally. Let's talk about how to put E+R=O into motion, starting today.

To learn more about the organization Andy Perkins founded and the outstanding work it does, visit **BESTWA.org**.

CONCLUSION:

TAKE A STEP

I'VE BEEN AROUND WATER most of my life. I took swimming lessons and was on a swim team as a child. Then, as you recall, I started working as a lifeguard in high school and, despite nearly getting fired, I eventually moved up to managing pools, certifying hundreds of lifeguards, and coaching swim teams.

Once I left the pool business in my mid-20s, I thought my coaching days were over. However, 15 years later, the Board of one of my former swim teams asked if I would consider coaching again. Even though I knew saying "yes" would require adding 35 extra hours to my workweek for three months each year, I couldn't resist diving back in. For the next seven summers, I was honored to coach the Steeple Station Stingrays—a team that ranged from

125 to 182 swimmers ages four to 18 (three of whom were my children). Every day, we learned lessons about competing and doing our best. We also learned about the importance of hard work, attitude, and sportsmanship. We even won a couple of divisional titles along the way.

As I look back on 13 years of coaching, several highlights stand out. I won't list them all, but the one that surprised me most is the realization that I have taught approximately 1,000 children how to swim. To clarify, this number doesn't reflect the number of children who took lessons from me—that's too high to count. No, this number represents the number of *non-swimming* children I taught to swim. That's a lot of time in the water with a lot of non-swimmers.

In retrospect, it's hard to remember the names and faces of most of these swimmers. First of all, keeping track of 1,000 children over 13 seasons (which actually spanned nearly 30 years) is no easy task. And second, as time marches on, my memories of these swimmers have blended together like a tropical smoothie. Maybe it's age, or perhaps the countless hours spent in the sun. Whatever the reason, most of these memories have now become a colorful, commingled swirl in my mind.

However...

There is one young swimmer who stands out. Since I worked with Shawn years ago, I have no doubt that some of my memories of him have blended with those of other swimmers. Still, the story you are about to read is true. And although I take a few liberties in retelling Shawn's story, I do so to draw attention to the emotional battle that raged within him. It's the same conflict that occurs inside most new swimmers. You see, Shawn's story is *everyone's story*.

So, who was Shawn, and why did he stand out?

Shawn was a freckled-faced little boy with matted hair who enrolled in swim lessons during my first year coaching. He stands out because his emotions were always front and center for the world to see. For instance, the first time I met Shawn, he walked onto the pool deck with a big, toothless grin and made an announcement that went something like this, "My name is Shawn, I'm four years old, and I hate the WAWA." I chuckled as Shawn sat down with the rest of the class. However, when I took him into the water for the first time, I quickly realized just how much he hated the "WAWA."

Let me pause the story here to let you in on two little secrets. First, Shawn's so-called "hatred" for the water wasn't really hatred. Yes, he was fearful, but he was also excited. As I mentioned, a conflict was raging inside Shawn. It's the same conflict taking place inside every child learning to swim. It's a tug-of-war between uncertainty and enthusiasm. For some children, this battle lasts only a day or two. For others, the emotional tugging and pulling can go on indefinitely.

The second little secret is this: teaching swimming isn't too complicated. It might not seem easy to most people because they only see uncoordinated arms and legs thrashing around in the water. However, learning to swim is pretty straightforward. There are two fundamental skills one must master. Once these two skills are learned, everything else falls into place.

The first skill is fundamental to getting your body into the proper position for swimming. To swim correctly, you must put your face in the water. If you don't, your rear end sinks, and you can't kick. Therefore, the only way to get your body into a prone or streamlined position (think flying like Superman through the water with your arms straight in front of you) is to put your face in the water.

The second skill is crucial for breathing while swimming. Once your face is in the water, you need to learn how to exhale while submerged. This is important because it prevents you from gasping for air when you turn your head to breathe. Instead, you only need to inhale when your mouth is above the water and exhale when it's submerged.

Even though swimming isn't complicated, you've probably guessed why children have such a difficult time learning to swim. It's because these two skills are scary. I can tell you from experience that four-, five-, and six-year-old children care very little about the science behind streamline swimming or exhaling underwater. I can also tell you that dunking a child's head underwater and holding it there until they blow bubbles isn't wise either. No, the best way to teach children these fundamental skills is to gamify things so that they learn to "hide their face in the water" and "blow bubbles." This approach goes a long way in helping new swimmers overcome their fears.

Now, back to the story.

Do you think instructing Shawn to "hide his face in the water" and "blow bubbles" did anything to subdue the tug-of-war going on inside him? Are you kidding me?! When I took Shawn into the water for the first time, his arms and legs wrapped around me like an octopus. He squeezed so tight, I couldn't breathe. All the while, he screamed at the top of his lungs, "My name is Shawn, I'm four years old, and I HATE THE WAWA!"

Pause again.

Here's another secret to let you in on. When teaching swimming, if you can convince children to do something they *think* is dangerous—but you *know* is safe—they not only start to trust you as their instructor, but their self-confidence skyrockets. That's why I ended every class by marching the kiddos down to the deep end and trying to convince them to jump off the diving board to me. If they did, it was like magic. Their confidence soared, and before you knew it, they were swimming across the pool.

Back to the story again.

The moment I used the phrase "diving board" in Shawn's presence…it was like a scene straight out of the movie *Twister*. Tables flipped and deck chairs went flying as this little guy sprinted straight to his mommy. (Yes, I'm exaggerating, but only slightly.)

During the next two weeks, Shawn learned nothing. He couldn't hide his face in the water. He couldn't blow bubbles. He could do one thing and one thing only—"My name is Shawn, I'm four years old, and I hate the WAWA."

When the next session of lessons rolled around, Shawn's mom asked if she could re-register him for the beginners' class. I said, "Sure." And that went on for almost two months. For two months, Shawn showed up to class with the same mix of apprehension and excitement. Yet every day, he couldn't get beyond, "My name is Shawn, I'm four years old, and I hate the WAWA."

Then, one day, completely out of the blue, Shawn came down to the deep end with the rest of the class. Not only that, but he crawled up on the diving board and walked to the end.

I was shocked! Here I was treading water, and for the first time, this freckle-faced boy was staring down at me. I encouraged him, "Come on, Shawn. You can do it! I'm so proud of you. Go ahead, buddy. Jump!"

And there he stood.

Eyes glued to the water.

Not a muscle moving.

Fifteen minutes later...

"Shawn, I'm going to drown. I cannot tread water forever. Come on, buddy. Jump."

That's when Shawn slowly turned around...cautiously walked to the back of the diving board...and climbed down. There was no jumping for Shawn that day.

The next day, the same thing happened, sparking a new trend. Day after day, Shawn walked to the end of the diving board. Day after day, I encouraged him to jump. And day after day, Shawn turned around and climbed off the diving board.

I'm embarrassed to admit this, but it got so bad that I started to ignore Shawn. He'd be in his usual position at the end of the diving board, and I'd be chatting it up with whoever was sitting in the lifeguard chair. On one particular day, a new, good-looking lifeguard was in the chair, and I said something like, "That's Shawn. He's four years old. He hates the WAWA. I'm Kent. I'm 21. I *love* the WAWA."

That's when I heard...

Bloop.

I looked up, and Shawn wasn't there.

I glanced around the pool deck, thinking, *Maybe he went to the Snack Bar or something.*

Eventually, I looked down and realized...

Shawn had jumped!

He was underwater, looking up at me with eyes the size of Hula Hoops.

And guess what? He was finally blowing bubbles—they were coming out of everywhere!

As I pulled him up out of the water, I half expected him to grab me by the neck and yell, "My name is Shawn. I'm four years old. I must terminate you!"

Instead, he looked me eyeball-to-eyeball and spat water in my face. Then, with a gigantic, toothless grin, he shouted, "I *looooove* the WAWA!"

During the next two weeks, Shawn learned more about swimming than he had in the previous two months. Was it because I'm such a great swim coach? Well, of course, but that's beside the point.

Shawn's confidence and swimming soared because he finally *took a step*.

SELF-HELP VERSUS SHELF-HELP

As stated at the beginning of the chapter, Shawn's story is everyone's story.

Actually, a better way to put this might be: Shawn's story *should be* everyone's story. That's because what we believe in is evidenced by the steps we take, not by the words we say.

The previous statement is a lot like sunscreen—for it to work, you have to rub it in. So let me say it again, this time with a few words highlighted to make sure it really sinks in: What we believe in is *evidenced* by the *steps* we take, *not* by the *words* we say.

People who read books like this do so to learn something new, and that's a good thing. However, learning something new is only half the goal. The other half, and the most crucial part, comes right now. It's the part where you decide to step into what you have learned and live it out. You see, there is a big difference between *learning* and *living*.

Learning is undoubtedly important. It's so essential that I have used the phrase "to learn, grow, and develop" throughout this book. But notice the two words that follow the first. *Grow* and *develop* describe the whole point of learning something new—to move it from your head to your heart and your hands. In this case, what good does it do to learn about E+R=O if you don't become like Shawn and step into what you've learned? Sure, taking 100 percent ownership of your life can be scary. But trust me, once you take that first step, your confidence will skyrocket. Within no time, you'll be "swimming across the pool" in how you live out E+R=O.

Think of it this way: If you take what you learn from this book and stick it on a shelf in your brain, that learning becomes *shelf-help* instead of *self-help*. Did you see what I did there? Yes, it's cheesy, but I hope it helps the idea stick because shelf-help does nothing for you. It's knowledge that just sits there and goes to waste. For new knowledge to mean anything, you have to put it into practice. It has to become a skill you use and develop. That's when it becomes self-help.

To wrap up this book, I'd like to share three daily habits that serve as self-help for me. When used together, they create TOMA for E+R=O, which stands for "Top-Of-Mind Awareness." In other words, regardless of what I face in life—whether adversity or good fortune—as long as I practice these habits, my built-in response is likely to be E+R=O.

THE 3 Rs FOR LIVING WHAT YOU BELIEVE

I call these habits my *3 Rs for Living*. Just as there are 3 Rs in learning (i.e., Reading, wRiting, and aRithmetic), there are also 3 Rs for living out what you believe.

HABIT 1: REV UP

The first thing I do in the morning is rev up my day, but it's probably not how you think.

Most people imagine "revving up" means "putting the pedal to the metal" the moment you crawl out of bed. But for me, it's the opposite. I slow down and *lead my life from quiet*.[1] That is to say, I spend 30 to 45 minutes at the start of the day practicing disciplines that anchor me to what is most important. I read my Bible and pray. I also read books on personal and professional development. I journal. I think about the Already, Not Yet character traits I want to build into my life. Finally, after leading my life from quiet, I use a simple daily planner that I created to map out the day ahead. If you'd like to see this planner (it's an easy system that takes about five minutes a day and uses just two pages of a 5"x7" spiral notebook), visit **KENTJULIAN.COM/RESPONSEBOOK** to take a look.

How does this habit help me live out E+R=O? While it slows me down on the outside, it has the opposite effect on the inside. When I start my day by taking time for personal development and focusing on what matters most, I get revved up! I feel energized and ready to dive into the day. This, in turn, helps me live a more Response-ABLE life.

So tomorrow, instead of rushing into your day like most people, why not start by leading your life from quiet? I think you'll find that nothing gets you more revved up for the day ahead than living on purpose and with purpose.

HABIT 2: REMINDERS

While the first habit helps you jumpstart your day with E+R=O, this one keeps you connected to E+R=O throughout the day. Plus, it's super easy to set up.

To make this habit work, place visual reminders of E+R=O in one or two places you will see during the day. For instance, some people write E+R=O on a Post-It Note and stick it to their bathroom mirror. Others have written it on a decorative rock and use it as a paperweight on their desk (and no, I don't believe Steve Meyer did this with his sapphire).

I have two E+R=O reminders that I see every day. The first is in my office. It's a decorative piece of wood on the wall with E+R=O painted on it. I see it every time I walk into my office.

The second, and my all-time favorite, is pictured on the next page. It's an E+R=O wristband that I wear at all times. I love this reminder because whenever I'm tempted to fall into E=O thinking, all I have to do is glance at my wrist to remind myself to be Response-ABLE. Trust me, this tool is powerful! It has kept me away from E=O behavior more times than I can count. (If you'd like to purchase E+R=O wristbands for yourself and/or your team, my company offers them in a variety of colors and sizes. You can find out more at **KENTJULIAN.COM/RESPONSEBOOK**.)

Take a Step

E+R=O Wristbands

HABIT 3: REVIEW

This last habit involves doing a simple check-in at the end of the day. And when I say "simple," I mean *simple*. You revved up your day early on by leading your life from quiet, so doing that again would be overkill. Plus, the goal here isn't to rev things back up; it's to ease things down and settle into the last part of your day. Therefore, you only need a few minutes to reflect on how you did at living E+R=O and whether you fell into any E=O pitfalls. That's it.

I do have one suggestion, though. The best time to practice this habit is at the end of your workday (or daily activities) and before reconnecting with your loved ones. There are two advantages to this. First, the habit naturally fits here—it's a tidy way to end that part of your day. Second, if your day has been rough, this habit helps you refocus on what truly matters. Many evenings, I've sat in my car for a few minutes before entering my home and whispered to myself, "The most important part of my day starts now. The people in this house are the ones I care about most. They deserve my time and attention. I need to be fully present."

STEP INTO WHAT YOU BELIEVE

From the very start of this book, I've made it clear that I'm an ordinary guy. No royal pedigree or superhuman talents. Just a fellow traveler who sometimes succeeds, sometimes struggles, and most often does a bit of both.

However, I also explained that I have extensive firsthand experience with the difference E+R=O can make. This experience comes from my own life and from seeing thousands of people positively impacted by this simple equation. You've had the chance to read some of my story, along with the stories of many of my friends. In each case, E+R=O has been the hero. It has instilled in us a strength of character that surpasses anything we inherited from our DNA. Furthermore, this simple mindset has given us an understanding of how the real world works (or at least how it works best). It has helped us build a foundation for success. And it has strengthened our grit.

Still, if all we did after learning about E+R=O was to stick it on a shelf, none of this would have happened. Each of us had to be Response-ABLE with what we learned. We had to choose to live E+R=O. Like Shawn, we had to take a step.

I'm often asked, "Is taking that step difficult? Is it hard to live out E+R=O?"

My answer to this is always the same.

"Yes and no."

Yes, living E+R=O is hard. It's hard to take 100 percent ownership of your life. It's hard to take charge of your attitude, associations, articulation, and actions. And it's especially hard to be Response-ABLE when the events you face are unpleasant, undesirable, or unfair.

But what's the alternative?

Learned helplessness?

A fixed mindset?

An E=O life?

You see, both E+R=O and E=O are hard. The difference is in the price you pay.

The price for E+R=O is an *investment* you pay *upfront*. The price for E=O is a *debt* that is collected *later*. So, while the cost of E+R=O may feel heavy at first, it produces abundant growth and lasting success. By contrast, E=O might offer temporary relief, but it eventually buries you under a debt you can never repay.

So yes, E+R=O is hard.

But by comparison?

It's not hard at all.

It all comes down to which price you're willing to pay and what kind of hard you want to step into.

A hard that shrinks your life?

Or a hard that expands your life?

I choose to step into the hard that expands my life. I've discovered it's a price worth paying. And I hope you choose the same.

Why?

Because E+R=O doesn't change your life in theory. It changes your life in motion.

So take a step. Then another. And then another.

And along the way, never forget that in every moment of every day, you're faced with events.

And your response?

That's what writes your story.

Bonus Chapter

E+R=O AND LEADERSHIP

BONUS CHAPTER:

E+R=O AND LEADERSHIP

LEADERSHIP MAGNIFIES EVERYTHING.

It multiplies your influence, your habits, your mindset—and yes, even your blind spots. But how you respond as a leader doesn't just shape your own outcomes; it sets the tone for everyone around you. That's why, if E+R=O is powerful in your personal life, it's absolutely mission-critical in leadership.

With that in mind, I would like to introduce you to Chris.

Chris's first job after college was a leadership role in an association with about 2,000 independent chapters across the United States. The chapter that hired him was small, and although he received other job offers, he chose this one because of the individual who hired him. What Chris appreciated most about his new boss was his character and high standards. Since Chris was young and inexperienced, he was more interested in learning from a quality leader than securing the "best" position or the highest-paying job. In the long run, he believed this would benefit his career. Looking back, he was right.

The work Chris was asked to do was challenging. He was starting a program from scratch with no staff and no budget. However, since his boss was a strong leader and mentor, Chris absorbed what he learned and made excellent progress.

Fast forward three years. The division Chris led experienced 10x growth. What started out as a one-person team grew to 11 strong, and the program they were building together continued to gain momentum.

Around this time, Chris was handpicked for a new national leadership initiative. Only 18 people were selected, and each was tasked with bringing the training back to their region. This validated the work Chris and his team were doing.

During the three days of training, Chris connected with a leader named Ed from the largest organization in their association. Chris wasn't looking for a job and didn't realize that Ed was trying to fill a position. However, as they networked and got to know each other, Ed suggested that Chris apply for the job.

Chris submitted his resume and waited. He waited and waited…and waited some more. He was eventually hired, and after a year in the new position, he discovered why the process had taken so long. Initially, the organization didn't want to hire Chris. Among all the candidates, he was the youngest and least qualified. However, after interviewing nearly a dozen people, they finally settled on him.

Looking back, this was Chris's best-case scenario. The Board of Directors believed their new hire had raw talent, but due to inexperience, they didn't expect much at first. And although Chris had achieved excellent results in his previous position, he was stepping into a program that was four or five times larger in scope. The Board's low expectations gave Chris enough breathing room to learn how to lead on a larger scale.

Fast forward again, and we discover it didn't take long before both parties realized how well things were working out. Within 18 months, Chris's team was experiencing better results than anyone expected. Things were going so well that the Board made Chris their youngest associate staff member ever. Year after year, he was given more responsibility and tasked with leading larger teams. And year after year, his teams achieved better results. It was as if he had a golden touch for leadership.

But then…something changed.

It happened so gradually that it went unnoticed at first. But looking back, it's clear what happened. All the success went to Chris's head. Instead of being confident, he became cocky. Not outwardly, but inwardly. And why not? Wasn't he the leader with the golden touch?

While all this was happening, Chris began searching for greener pastures. He was now a nationally recognized leader within his industry, which meant other organizations sought him out. Practically every month, a new job offer landed on his desk. So, when he finally decided to move on, he got to pick exactly where he wanted to go. Ultimately, he chose what he believed was the perfect organization in the perfect location. Although Chris was only in his early 30s, he was about to experience the pinnacle of his career.

And then...

He crashed and burned.

After an initial hero's welcome to his new role, things quickly turned sour. Not because the organization was the problem—Chris was. His perspective had shifted during the final years in his previous job. He now believed his success came from his golden touch as a leader, rather than recognizing much of it came from the privilege of growing, developing, and leading a great team. Together, they achieved outstanding results, and he became a better leader along the way. But now, he was arrogant. This young leader—once wise beyond his years—had lost his way. Success had gone to his head, and he believed he was the main reason behind most of it.

This attitude ultimately led to his downfall, which happened quickly once he landed in his new position. He had been at his previous job for years, but this one lasted only nine months. He came in as a hero but left as a heel.

Over the next several years, Chris became a shell of the man and leader he once was. The disappointment he felt in himself and his performance was paralyzing. Yet these feelings didn't just affect him professionally; they also impacted his personal life. For instance, his wife had a front-row seat to everything, and she was now watching her husband wrestle with insecurity and doubt she had never seen before. And although she was concerned for him, she was also losing confidence in him.

During those tumultuous years, something Chris's wife said finally brought clarity. Chris had been told his future boss could be tough to work for, so she asked if this concerned him. To this day, he is embarrassed by his response. He smugly said, "Well, it won't be a problem for me because this man has never worked with a leader like me." Chris's wife said, "That's when I knew your heart had changed."

And she was right. Instead of remembering the E+R=O lessons he had learned from his mentors, everything was now about how wonderful *he* was as a leader. He had forgotten that growing, developing, and leading a Response-ABLE team is the ultimate privilege for a leader. He also forgot that humility, not just confidence, was essential to being that kind of leader.

THE GREATEST THREAT TO LEADERSHIP

The greatest threat to leadership isn't failure—it's success. Why? Because if you're not careful, you may start believing your own press clippings:

- "You're such an amazing leader."
- "We couldn't have accomplished this without you."
- "Your vision is what turned the company around."

Even if these compliments are sincere, they're one-dimensional. But leadership isn't one-dimensional. It's not even multi-dimensional. It's multi-, multi-, multi-dimensional.

Chris's story vividly illustrates this. As a young man, he was mentored by several E+R=O leaders, and these leaders gave him an incredible advantage. It wasn't that Chris was more gifted than other young leaders—he simply understood the importance of building E+R=O teams. The more he leaned into that vision, the better he led and the more Response-ABLE his teams became. This was Chris's advantage!

Although Chris began with that leadership vision, success eventually went to his head. He forgot the E+R=O lessons he learned from his mentors and started to believe he was the reason good things happened (which is classic one-dimensional thinking). This misguided belief led him in the opposite direction from where he started. Instead of being an E+R=O leader who invested in his team, he adopted an E=O mindset. That is to say, he began seeing his "great" leadership as the *event* and assumed this meant he would always experience successful *outcomes*.

But ultimately, E=O did what it always does. It caused Chris's life and leadership to shrink. And it didn't stop there. The repercussions rippled through the organization and the people he led. As I stated at the beginning of the chapter, *leadership magnifies everything*.

WE REPRODUCE WHO WE ARE

As you know, the purpose of this book is to equip you to proactively choose an E+R=O mindset rather than passively surrendering to E=O. While I haven't focused heavily on leadership throughout the book, the fingerprints of effective leadership are all over the previous pages. That's why I decided to include this Bonus Chapter—to expand on what you've read and share a few additional insights about E+R=O and leadership.

Here are two quick thoughts to help you get the most out of this Bonus Chapter. First, I won't waste your time repeating ideas

I've already shared. Although I build on previous concepts, most ideas in this chapter are new and, more importantly, specific to leadership. Second, in order to stay focused on the role E+R=O plays in leadership, one overriding leadership principle will inform every point I make: "We teach what we know, but we reproduce who we are."

Just as in our personal life, being an effective E+R=O leader originates from the inside out. In other words, what you do as a leader always begins with who you are. As the success principle from earlier puts it: "Your DOING flows out of your BEING."

Interestingly, however, no one learns E+R=O this way, at least not at first. We don't learn it from the inside out; we learn it from the *outside in*. That's how we learn everything. We're exposed to information and knowledge *outside* ourselves (like this book, for instance). We then process that information *inside* ourselves. Finally, we decide whether or not to apply what we have learned to our lives. Again, learning begins from the outside in.

That's why the leadership principle I just mentioned is so crucial. As leaders, we teach what we know, *but we reproduce who we are*. For this reason, if you are a leader, just telling your team how to live E+R=O isn't enough. They must *see* you living it! They have to observe how E+R=O gets fleshed out in the messiness of life. Otherwise, it won't stick.

With this in mind, here are several character traits and leadership skills that enable leaders to live out E+R=O. The character traits are *inner qualities* that will keep you centered as a leader. The leadership skills are *outer competencies* that will help you lead others forward.

INNER QUALITIES OF AN E+R=O LEADER

E+R=O LEADERS PUT CHARACTER FIRST

As mentioned on the previous page (and throughout this book), E+R=O works from the inside out. In other words, the more this mindset becomes an integral part of who you are and how you're wired (i.e., your being), the more it influences how you respond to events (i.e., your doing). This is why E+R=O leaders prioritize their own character development above all else.

I was fortunate to have been mentored by several successful leaders early in my career. While their talent initially caught my eye, I knew there was more to them than talent. Something else made them stand out. Around that time, I read about the difference between the "Personality Ethic" and the "Character Ethic," which helped me understand what made these leaders unique.

According to Stephen Covey, most literature on success during the first 150 years of the United States focused on what he calls the "Character Ethic." Qualities like "integrity, humility, fidelity, temperance, courage, justice, patience, industry, simplicity, modesty, and the Golden Rule" were regarded as foundational for success.

However, shortly after World War I, Covey argues that the focus of success shifted to the "Personality Ethic." This approach emphasizes strategies like communication skills, influence techniques, and other similar methods. It's not that the Personality Ethic isn't beneficial; we should all strive to improve our communication and influence. However, according to Covey (and I agree), the Personality Ethic should be secondary. The primary ethic for success is character.[1]

This is where Chris got things wrong. He started out as an E+R=O leader, but over time, he neglected to prioritize his character. This led to a reliance on external techniques rather than internal traits. Yet, as any good leader knows, character is the cornerstone of leadership. It is the key to building trust. No matter how effective your outward techniques may be, you will never succeed as a leader if your foundation is weak. That's why E+R=O leaders put character first and prioritize it above all else.

E+R=O LEADERS SEE THEMSELVES AS GUIDES

In his book *The Hero with a Thousand Faces*, Joseph Campbell explains how every "Hero's Journey" follows the same basic outline:

- The Hero character faces a challenge.
- Along the way, that character meets a Guide (i.e., mentor).
- To help the Hero overcome the challenge, the Guide shows the Hero a path to follow and calls that character to action.
- The rest of the story chronicles the ordeals and trials the Hero faces as they attempt to overcome the challenge and achieve success.[2]

These two characters—the Hero and the Guide—appear in virtually every hero movie today:

- In *Spider-Man*, Peter Parker is the Hero, and Uncle Ben is the Guide.
- In *Wonder Woman*, Diana is the Hero, and Steve Trevor is the Guide.
- In *The Matrix*, Neo is the Hero, and Morpheus is the Guide.
- And, of course, in the original *Star Wars*, Luke Skywalker is the Hero, and Obi-Wan Kenobi is the Guide.

Interestingly, these two characters can also be seen in the "Hero's Journey" of leadership. However, while many leaders view themselves as Heroes, the best leaders recognize they are Guides. And this distinction, more than any other, helps E+R=O leaders understand the true nature of servant leadership.

For most people, the term "servant leadership" implies that leaders are willing to serve their team by performing tasks that others would rather not do. This isn't necessarily a bad definition; it's just simplistic. As you recall from our discussion of the Simplicity Bell Curve, we are all novices when we learn something new. That means our understanding, while likely accurate, is basic and superficial. However, there is a deeper, more profound, and even truer simplicity on the far side of the bell curve—one that is more meaningful and useful.

Keeping this in mind, a deeper and more helpful understanding of servant leadership recognizes that the best way for leaders to serve their team is to empower them to be Heroes of their own stories. Just as Obi-Wan Kenobi taught Luke Skywalker to use the Force to guide his path, we should teach our team members to use E+R=O to navigate their own lives. It's not that they will never need our help or direction; they probably will at some point. However, adopting the approach of guiding team members (instead of trying to be their Hero) promises to give them greater confidence in themselves and their capabilities. Ultimately, this approach serves those we lead best, and that's the true essence of servant leadership.

E+R=O LEADERS EMBRACE HEALTHY TENSIONS

Lastly, the most effective E+R=O leaders are those who embrace character traits that may initially seem contradictory. These paradoxes can create inner tension, but it's a healthy tension that promotes growth and balance. For instance, E+R=O leaders tend to:

- Be driven, yet patient
- Be bold, yet considerate
- Hold strong convictions, yet remain curious

There are many other internal paradoxes, but the one that stands out as most important for E+R=O leaders is the balance between *confidence* and *humility*.

When it comes to the healthy tension between confidence and humility, most people are unlikely to follow a leader who lacks confidence. At the same time, if you aren't humble enough to admit you don't have all the answers, no one will follow you either. It's not hard to understand why these two things are true. Confidence without humility leads to pride, while humility without confidence results in doubt and second-guessing. Therefore, as a leader, it's essential to master both.

While both traits are critical to leadership, humility warrants a bit of extra attention, as many leaders find it especially challenging to embrace. The truth is, only humble leaders care. Only humble leaders forgive. And only humble leaders serve sacrificially. At the same time, staying humble is an ongoing battle even for healthy leaders. It requires openness to feedback, adaptability, and the willingness to admit when you're wrong. All of this points to a simple truth: humility isn't a one-time achievement; it's an ongoing pursuit.

Again, this is where Chris went wrong. Instead of striking a balance between confidence and humility, all the success went to his head. He became cocky—not outwardly, but inwardly. Over time, he lost his way and began to believe he had all the answers.

The bottom line is this: mastering the healthy tension between confidence and humility will be a lifelong pursuit for you as a leader. But it will also be one of the main reasons why people choose to follow you.

OUTER COMPETENCIES OF AN E+R=O LEADER

Now that we've explored several inner qualities that define *who* E+R=O leaders are, let's look at a few outer competencies that influence *how* E+R=O leaders lead.

E+R=O LEADERS EMPOWER PEOPLE WHO ARE IN PROCESS

Over the years, I've met several leaders who have said, "I love my job. It's the people I can do without." My response is always the same: "Why in the world are you in leadership?!"

I understand their frustration. Some people are difficult to lead. However, it's crucial to remember that most people are in process. They want to do their jobs well, and many are growing on the inside more than we realize—they just aren't showing it.

So yes, it's true that leaders sometimes have to deal with individuals who are not interested in learning, growing, and developing. All they want is a paycheck and to be left alone. And frankly, if someone doesn't want to be there and couldn't care less about improving, the best thing leaders can do for that person and the organization is to be honest and part ways. You're not helping anyone by keeping them around.

Having said that, most team members are in process, and your role as a leader is to guide them toward success (remember, you want them to be the Heroes of their stories). An excellent way to do this is with a strategy we discussed earlier: Already, Not Yet statements. Although I previously shared this strategy, the focus was on your own personal growth. As a leader, however, you can also use it to propel others forward.

As a reminder, an Already, Not Yet statement is a positive proclamation that a person *already* believes and wants to be true about their life. However, if they are honest, it is *not yet* a reality.

With this in mind, one of your roles as a leader is to be a talent scout who looks for character traits and skills in individuals that they may not recognize in themselves. When you see these qualities in someone, it's your job to highlight them. The easiest way to do this is by sharing an Already, Not Yet statement. For instance, you might say something like this (filling in the blank with what you see in a person):

> I've noticed you want to do well in
> your work, and I appreciate that about you.
> I have also noticed something else.
> I believe you are the type of person who can
> _____.

Not only will doing this inspire the person, but it will also naturally lead to a conversation about how that person can apply the character trait or skill in their job. Moving forward, you can follow up with periodic check-ins to nurture motivation and accountability for their continued development.

I have used Already, Not Yet statements when mentoring teenagers, coaching swimmers, working with employees, consulting leaders, and even with my own children. It is one of the best leadership tools I know of because it creates personal motivation by elevating an individual's vision of who they can be. But it doesn't stop there; it also fosters determination as they pursue that vision. When I look back at my early mentors, every single one of them used this strategy with me, whether they had a name for it or not. They helped me see personal traits and talents that I would have never recognized. My life is better because of what they helped me see!

Before moving on, there is one more thing to remember about people in process. Just as you need the freedom to briefly slip back into E=O thinking when things get tough, your people need that freedom, too. Therefore, don't be such an E+R=O fanatic that you never allow others the chance to express their frustrations. Let them occasionally vent about unfair treatment or what went wrong. Once their grievances are on the table, you can guide them back into taking charge of their response relatively quickly.

E+R=O LEADERS VIEW PERFORMANCE THROUGH AN E+R=O PARADIGM

You've probably read statistics like:

- High performers make up 20 percent of an organization
- Average performers make up 60 percent
- Poor performers make up 20 percent

Whether these statistics are accurate or not doesn't really matter. What matters is that they hinder leadership's influence right from the start. That's because they automatically shape a leader's perception by placing people on different "rungs" of the performance ladder. Even worse, these statistics can demotivate team members by casting doubt on their potential.

Here's a better approach for assessing performance. Instead of comparing top performers with underperformers, why not use E+R=O for evaluation? In this case, the percentages might look like this:

- Individuals who consistently live E+R=O make up 20 percent of the organization

- Individuals making progress in E+R=O make up 60 percent
- Members who are stuck in E=O make up 20 percent

How does this paradigm enhance your leadership influence? Simple. It creates more (and better) opportunities to inspire and equip people in E+R=O. This occurs in various ways, but here are three examples.

First, it establishes a common language and accountability around the E+R=O mindset. This is important because, when leadership does a better job of explaining and demonstrating E+R=O, more people begin to embody it. As this happens, the percentage at the top of the paradigm can increase. That means there is no reason it can't reach 40 percent, 50 percent, or more. How awesome would that be for your organization?!

Second, an E+R=O framework enhances a team's performance by *not* focusing directly on performance. I know that sounds counterintuitive, but it's true. As you recall, when people are Response-ABLE, they take ownership of their attitude, associations, articulation, and actions. The more capable they become at doing this, the more these areas expand for them and the better they perform. On the other hand, when leaders prioritize performance above everything else, the focus on people's attitude, associations, articulation, and actions diminishes. Over time, this unconscious emphasis on "doing" over "being" is likely to erode the integrity of individuals and the organization. The bottom line is this: the best way for leaders to enhance performance (i.e., doing) and integrity (i.e., being) is to prioritize E+R=O. Do this, and performance takes care of itself.

Third, the E+R=O paradigm also serves as an antidote to the accusation of favoritism. That's because leaders will be enthusiastic about *everyone* who makes progress in applying E+R=O!

E+R=O LEADERS RUN AT CHALLENGES

Finally, when faced with a challenge, leaders have three options. They can run *at* the challenge. They can run *away* from it. Or they can attempt to run *around* it. E+R=O leaders should always, and I mean always, run *at* challenges.

Before we dive into what it means to run at a challenge, let's examine the two other options. First, you won't last long as a leader if you run away from challenges. There is nothing more to be said here; it's just that simple.

Second, running around problems isn't leadership either. It's cowardice at best, and deceitful and manipulative at worst. Strong words, I know, but this approach is more akin to playing politics than leading. For example, when I was asked to lead an additional division within an organization, it took less than a nanosecond to discover that one of the previous leaders had intentionally worked around his team for years (deceitful). Talk about a mess! There was zero trust, people were territorial, and each "side" did its own thing. One day, I called this former leader to ask why he led this way. He said, "It was easier to get things done." When I explained the dysfunction I was facing, he laughed and said it was the same when he was there. Then, word-for-word, he said, "I just worked around those people" (manipulative). Needless to say, cleaning up that mess was nasty, and several people lost their jobs. They weren't bad people, but for over a decade, they had been ignored by leadership, and trust had eroded completely. The previous leader had worked *around* them, not *through* them, leaving a permanent scar that never fully healed. No matter what I said or did, they simply didn't trust me because I was in charge.

So, what does it mean to run at challenges? Frankly, it's the epitome of E+R=O leadership because it aligns with every section of this book. First, running at challenges means you deal with *reality* head-on by gathering the facts about the situation, the people involved, and the decisions that need to be made. Second, you determine what it will take to achieve *success* by looking for opportunities and solutions even if the circumstances are less than ideal. Finally, you realize the path ahead will likely require *grit*, but no matter how hard it is or how long it takes, you and your team are committed to running at the challenge until you figure out the best way forward. It won't always be easy, and it won't always be pretty, but it's always the best option for E+R=O leaders.

THE REST OF THE STORY

Let's wrap things up by revisiting Chris's story. I have no way of knowing if his story resonates with you, but it certainly does with me. That's because my name is Christopher Kent Julian, and that's my story.

Sharing this part of my life with you is both embarrassing and rewarding. It's embarrassing because I'm painfully aware of how far I drifted from where I started. In many ways, I dishonored the mentors who invested in me early on. I was fortunate to be guided by several remarkable leaders when I first started out, but during that season, I allowed my ego to overshadow the lessons they had taught me.

I'm also ashamed of dropping the ball and disappointing so many people. The organization that hired me expected great things, and instead of showing up with my "A" game, I didn't even function at a "C-" level.

Yet, in a strange way, sharing this part of my life is also rewarding because that season, unlike any other, shaped me into a better person and leader. It humbled me, and that humiliation lingers at the forefront of my mind. Not in a debilitating way, but in an inspiring way. I find myself remembering those days and saying, "Never again!"

"Never again will I allow arrogance to prevent me from listening to others."

"Never again will I believe that I am somehow special and more important than others."

"And never again will I lose focus on the one thing I am in charge of—my response."

As mentioned at the beginning of the chapter, leadership magnifies everything. That's why I made sure everything we discussed here was shaped by the one leadership principle I believe is most important to remember: "We teach *what* we know, but we reproduce *who* we are." Today, as someone who is once again striving to be an E+R=O leader, I hope my story, along with the leadership lessons I shared, reproduces in you the wisdom needed to avoid the mistakes I made.

Additionally, I'll leave you with one final thought…

Wise leaders learn from their own mistakes, but the wisest leaders learn from the mistakes of others. While many leaders fall into the first group, only E+R=O leaders consistently belong to the second group.

Make sure you are a member of Group Number Two!

AFTERWORD:

OUCH!

Every spring, I scalp my lawn.

If you don't live in a region like the Southeastern United States, you've probably never heard of "scalping" your lawn. It's the practice of mowing your yard as low as possible at the start of the growing season. Here's how the Lawn Doctor® describes it: "Scalping is mostly suitable for warm-season grasses like Bermuda grass. This is because these types of grasses go dormant during the winter and require a boost to start growing again in the spring."[1]

Important things to remember when scalping are:

- **Timing** — Scalping should only be done in early spring. Doing it at any other time will damage your lawn.

- **Ouch** — If grass could speak, it would shout, "Ouch!" because you're cutting it as low as possible. Case in point, I fill 20 yard-waste bags with grass clippings when scalping; a typical mowing only fills one or two.
- **Purposeful** — The purpose of scalping is to get rid of dead thatch and worthless debris.
- **Growth** — Scalping encourages healthy growth and a stronger, more beautiful yard.

As you look back over your life, have you noticed that most of your significant growth occurred during "scalping" seasons? I sure have. And believe it or not, while I was bagging mounds and mounds of dead grass this past spring, I got to thinking about this. I had been busy putting the finishing touches on this book, so my mind naturally drifted to several difficult "scalping" seasons from my past. What I realized was:

- **Timing** — The timing was always right. Scalping occurred during seasons when I had serious blind spots that needed to be addressed.
- **Ouch** — Unlike grass, I can speak, and I did say, "Ouch!"
- **Purposeful** — Although the process was painful, I can now look back and see the dead, worthless debris that needed to be cut out of my life. Bagging it up and throwing it out was a good thing.
- **Growth** — Like most people, I wish I didn't have to go through such painful experiences. Still, I'm grateful for the healthy growth each one produced.

In light of this analogy, I'd like to share two final thoughts. These are personal thoughts about who I am and what matters most to me.

As a professional speaker and leadership consultant, I aim to help organizations (1) build resilient teams and (2) cultivate Response-ABLE cultures. It probably comes as no surprise that my keynote presentations focus on E+R=O and the ideas outlined in this book. However, as someone who embraces a biblical worldview, it may surprise you to learn that I do not share about my faith in presentations—unless specifically requested to do so by the decision maker in charge. The reason is simple: I am hired to speak and train on a specific leadership topic, and a person's religious beliefs does not affect their ability to understand or apply E+R=O. Therefore, since I am hired to equip people in E+R=O, that's what I do.

That being said, since this book is a personal project, I'd like to share a personal belief that I don't share in presentations. I believe the Bible gives me a deeper, more profound, and truer understanding of E+R=O, which helps me live it out more effectively. Why do I say that? Because while my role in E+R=O is to own my response, the Bible teaches that God is in charge of events. Therefore, the more I learn to trust God, the better I can understand how He uses events in my life for my good and His purposes.

For example, Romans 8:28 is a verse in the Bible that states, "And we know that God causes all things to work together for good to those who love God, to those who are called according to His purpose."[2] Using the scalping analogy to think more deeply about this verse:

- **Timing** — God's timing is perfect, and if we choose to love Him, He will providentially cause all things to work together for our good.
- **Ouch** — Yes, adversity and difficulties are painful, but again, God causes all things—even painful events—to work together for our good if we love Him.
- **Purposeful** — If we choose to love God, He purposely causes each event we experience to happen *for* us and not just to us.
- **Growth** — Romans 8:28 insinuates that God's good work in our lives is for our growth, but another verse tells us more clearly that "He [God] who began a good work in us will perfect it until the day of Jesus Christ."[3]

Can you see why I say the Bible teaches that God is in charge of events? Can you also see why this truth encourages me? If God is sovereign and in control of all events (which is what the Bible teaches), and if He is good, just, merciful, and trustworthy (also what the Bible teaches), then I trust Him to follow through on His promise to use every event in my life for my good and His purposes. What an amazing, overwhelming, staggering truth!

What, then, is my response?

For one, I am grateful. I have done nothing and can do nothing to deserve such a gift.

But two, as someone who has put my trust in God, I am committed to doing my part and responding to events in a way that honors Him. This is especially important during "scalping" seasons, because those moments are when I need to trust that He is causing all things to work together for my good and His purposes—even if I am saying, "Ouch!"

One final thought. The subtitle of this book states that E+R=O is the *only* mindset for success, and from a human standpoint, that is true. As I've shared, E+R=O is an umbrella under which all success principles fall, and if you read the biblical Book of Proverbs, you will see the fingerprints of E+R=O on practically every verse in that book. In other words, even the Bible views E+R=O as the only mindset for achieving excellence in this life.

However, from an eternal perspective, true success is about much more than achievements and accomplishments, and Jesus teaches that true fulfillment and ultimate success are only found in Him. That is why He made hard statements such as, "For what does it benefit a person to gain the whole world, and forfeit his soul?"[4]

In Chapter Three, I explained that the best purpose statement acts like a compass that points to true north. Not my opinion or your opinion of true north, but *the* true north. With this in mind, if the Bible is what it claims to be—if it is God's divine revelation to humanity—then it points to *the* true north. This means discovering what it says about who God is, what He has done for us, and who we can be in Him is what real success is ultimately all about.

Therefore, while E+R=O is the only mindset for success from a human standpoint, the same holds true from a heavenly perspective. The most significant *event* in history—the death and resurrection of Jesus Christ—and our *response* to it determine our eternal *outcome*. As Jesus said in John 10:10, "I came that you may have life, and have it abundantly."[5] That's why choosing to follow Him leads to ultimate and everlasting success.

If you're interested in learning more about the Bible and what it says about who God is, what He has done for us, and who we can be in Him, visit **LiveItForward.com/BiblicalResources** for additional resources or use the QR code below. (Please note, this link is different from the other resource links shared throughout the book.)

ACKNOWLEDGMENTS

No book is published solely by the author. The time, energy, and effort invested by others often exceeds what most can imagine. I am deeply grateful to those who have helped bring this book to life.

To my family—especially my wife, Kathy, and our three children, Chris, McKenzie, and Kelsey—your love and support through the years has been invaluable. Although you weren't directly involved in the writing, editing, or publishing (aside from McKenzie), you have had a front-row seat to my journey of learning to live and lead with an E+R=O mindset. Thank you for your unwavering patience and encouragement through the years.

To the leaders and mentors who have invested in me, particularly Jim Vaught, Dan Glaze, Dan Hettinger, Bob Thune, Rich Gianacakos, and Dan Miller—much of this book is rooted in the lessons I have learned from watching your lives. I am deeply grateful for your guidance and the role you have played in shaping my life.

To the Board and volunteer youth staff at Christ Community Church—my eight years with you were pivotal in my growth from an E+R=O novice to an E+R=O leader. The lessons and memories remain both enduring and cherished.

To McKenzie Julian, Bobby McGraw, and James Woosley—your expertise in editing, word-smithing, and publishing has been an absolute gift. Thank you for your support.

And to all the audiences I have had the privilege of speaking to—past and future—I consider it an honor to share the E+R=O message with you.

NOTES

INTRODUCTION: THE GIFT

1. Our first French Bulldog was actually named Techie. However, since he was a black-and-brown brindle, black-and-white photos of him don't show up well in print. Additionally, Kathy considers both French Bulldogs to be the best gift she ever received from me.

CHAPTER 1: MORE THAN A PAPERWEIGHT

1. John Harmon, "Sapphire Found in N.C. May Bring Pair Fortune," *The Toccoa Record* (n.d.).
2. These are the letters listed on a report my parents received from a speech therapist when I was in first grade.
3. I use this "DNA" analogy throughout the book. To be clear, I am not suggesting that E=O or E+R=O are literally part of a person's DNA (Deoxyribonucleic Acid). Rather, the analogy illustrates how your mindset can become deeply ingrained in your identity and eventually become an integral part of who you are. For example, just as DNA contains the code that determines how living organisms grow, function, and respond to their environment, adopting an E+R=O mindset means your Responses (*R*) become the key factor in how you adapt to Events (*E*) and shape your Outcomes (*O*). In contrast, adopting an E=O mindset is akin to having "contaminated mental DNA," where your Outcomes (*O*) are primarily shaped by the Events (*E*) you face.

4. A technical argument could be made that there is no such thing as E=O because everyone "responds" to the events that happen to them. While factually accurate, this argument overlooks the underlying purpose of using the two equations to represent distinct mindsets. Each equation illustrates what a person chooses to empower in their life. People with an E+R=O mindset choose to empower their *responses*, whereas people with an E=O mindset choose to passively accept whatever *events* happen to them.

5. Martin E. P. Seligman, *Learned Optimism: How to Change Your Mind and Your Life* (New York: Books, 2006), 15.

6. Ibid., 113. These are symptoms from a bullet point list. Additional symptoms are shared throughout the book.

7. Ibid, 40-48. These pages thoroughly describe the meaning of the words in quotation marks.

8. Stephen R. Covey, *The 7 Habits of Highly Effective People: Restoring The Character Ethic* (New York: Fireside, 1989), 71.

9. Jack Canfield, *The Success Principles: How to Get from Where You Are to Where You Want to Be* (New York: HarperCollins, 2005), 3.

10. Ibid.

CHAPTER 2: THE WAY WE VIEW THINGS IS THE WAY WE DO THINGS

1. Fred Hartley, *What's Right What's Wrong In An Upside Down World* (Nashville: Thomas Nelson Inc, 1988), 26. After researching these claims, I believe this story is about experiments done by psychologist George M. Stratton (1865-1957). However, Stratton's studies inspired many other similar studies, so it is impossible to determine whether this story is specific to Stratton's work or someone who followed in his footsteps.

2. Malcolm Gladwell, *David and Goliath: Underdogs, Misfits, and the Art of Battling Giants* (New York: Little, Brown and Company, 2013), 5.

3. Ibid., 6.

4. Ibid., 5.

5. When referring to my teenage, college, and early career years, I use adjectives like "essence," "basics," and "concept" to describe my understanding of E+R=O. This is because, while I was learning and growing in my ability to be Response-ABLE, I had not yet been introduced to the E+R=O equation. As you recall, that formal introduction came nearly 20 years after my basketball coach, Jim Vaught, first introduced me to the concept. He was the one who

initially taught me that my outcomes could be shaped by my responses and not just by the events I experienced. So, while I hadn't yet heard of E+R=O, I already had a foundational grasp of the mindset behind it.

6. I have used this phrase for years in leadership training, and while I don't believe it's original with me, I'm unsure of its origins. I searched online to see if it was attributed to anyone, but found no source material.

CHAPTER 3: WHAT IS SUCCESS?

1. John C. Maxwell, *Developing the Leader Within You* (Nashville: Thomas Nelson Inc., 1993), 31.
2. Stephen R. Covey, *First Things First* (New York: Simon & Schuster, 1994), 75.
3. Covey, *7 Habits*, 98.
4. David Brooks, *The Road to Character* (New York: Random House, 2015), xi.
5. Covey, *7 Habits*, 98.
6. Years ago, I came across this story by Robert W. Sutton in a magazine. I photocopied the story, but regretfully, I did not document the magazine.
7. Logically, for a purpose statement to function as a compass, it must point to true north. That is to say, the answers to the "Being" and "Doing" questions must be built upon a "One Thing" that is objectively true. An objective truth is something that is always true, whether we choose to believe it or not. Compare this to a subjective truth, which is more of an opinion than a fact. Subjective truths are based on personal feelings, opinions, or beliefs, which means even when we sincerely believe them, we can be sincerely wrong. In other words, I might believe "my truth" is true, but if it is not objectively true, no matter how sincere I am, I could still be basing my belief on something that is a lie. Personally, my greatest endeavor in life is to seek "the truth" rather than "my truth." This means I strive to objectively discover, outside of myself, what is true, good, noble, pure, right, and virtuous.
8. These purpose statements come from client worksheets in rough draft form. Therefore, several statements include minor editorial changes. These changes were for grammatical purposes only, none of which changes the statements' meaning.

CHAPTER 4: THE EXPANDING FENCE POSTS

1. Goodreads (n.d.), Oliver Wendell Holmes Quotes, accessed 30 July 2024, <https://www.goodreads.com/author/quotes/1203736.Oliver_Wendell_Holmes_Sr_>.
2. Quote Fancy (n.d.), *Top 500 Albert Einstein Quotes (2023 Update)*, accessed 20 November 2023, <https://quotefancy.com/albert-einstein-quotes>. According to Alice Calaprice, the editor of *The Ultimate Quotable Einstein* (Princeton, Princeton University Press, 2011), the quote starting with "Everything should be made as simple as possible..." is a compressed version of lines from a lecture given by Einstein at Oxford University on June 10, 1933.

CHAPTER 5: IT'S A BIG UMBRELLA!

1. Hartley, *Upside Down World*, 20.
2. Covey, *7 Habits*, 35.
3. Ibid.
4. Goodreads (n.d.), *Jodie Foster Quotes*, accessed 11 April 2024, <https://www.goodreads.com/author/quotes/1228762.Jodie_Foster>.
5. Brian Tracy, *Million Dollar Habits: Proven Power Practices to Double and Triple Your Income* (Irvine: Entrepreneur Press, 2017), 10.
6. Lee Ellis, *Leading With Honor: Leadership Lessons from the Hanoi Hilton* (Cumming, GA: FreedomStar Media, 2012), XIII.

CHAPTER 6: A WHOLE LOTTA ELVIS GOIN' ON

1. *Modelling Elvis Impersonators*, accessed 22 October 2024, <https://www.slideserve.com/aria/modelling-elvis-impersonators>.
2. While it is difficult to find books that focus exclusively on grit, many personal and professional development books discuss the concept. A few of my favorites, in addition to Angela Duckworth's *Grit*, include *David and Goliath* by Malcolm Gladwell, *Learned Optimism* by Martin E. P. Seligman, *Atomic Habits* by James Clear, and *Mindset* by Carol Dweck.
3. Angela Duckworth, *Grit: The Power of Passion and Perseverance* (New York: Scribner, 2016), 8.
4. The singular and plural forms of "muscle" are used interchangeably when speaking about the muscle behind grit. This is not meant to

confuse the reader. Most works that explain the muscular system take a similar approach. In fact, both the singular and plural forms of the word "muscle" are often used interchangeably when referring to more technical terms like "muscle fibers," "muscle tissues," "muscle types," and even "organs." I take the same approach in this book. To clarify, I view the E+R=O mindset as a singular muscle that strengthens a person's grit in two ways. First, it functions as a "heartbeat muscle" regarding the passion and direction side of grit. Second, it also functions as a "behavioral muscle" in terms of the perseverance and determination side of grit.

5. *Facts About Blood*, accessed 3 December 2024, <https://www.hopkinsmedicine.org/health/wellness-and-prevention/facts-about-blood>.

6. YouTube (n.d.), *One Question To Transform Anyone's Future — Multiplier Mindset*, accessed 14 July 2025, <https://www.youtube.com/watch?v=N9hwVNcHz9c>. I was initially introduced to the Dan Sullivan Question during a 48 Days Mastermind retreat (I do not recall which one, so I cannot give an exact date). This video, or one similar to it, was played during that event.

7. Carol S. Dweck, Ph.D, *Mindset: The New Psychology of Success* (New York: Ballantine Books, 2016), 6.

8. Ibid., 7.

9. Ibid.

10. Duckworth, *Grit*, 54.

11. Ibid., 117.

CHAPTER 7: MUSCLE UP (WITHOUT STEROIDS)

1. Gary Gulbranson, *Leadership* (Carol Stream: Christianity Today, Summer 1989), 43.

2. Duckworth, *Grit: The power of passion and perseverance*, April 2013, TED Talks Education <https://www.ted.com/talks/angela_lee_duckworth_grit_the_power_of_passion_and_perseverance?subtitle=en>.

3. All information and statistics are from BESTWA's *Year in Review 2024* Newsletter.

4. Jeanette Settembre, March 9, 2023, *I Always Looked Different Than the Rest of My Family—Turns Out I Was Switched at Birth*, accessed 25 February 2025, <https://nypost.com/2023/03/09/man-discovers-he-was-a-baby-switched-at-birth-after-dna-test>.

CONCLUSION: TAKE A STEP

1. I heard this phrase years ago, but cannot remember who said it.

BONUS CHAPTER: E+R=O AND LEADERSHIP

1. Covey, *7 Habits*, 18-23.
2. Joseph Campbell, *The Hero with a Thousand Faces* (Princeton: Princeton University Press, 1968).

* To preserve my identity in the opening story until the end of the chapter, I used my first name instead of my middle name (which is the name I go by), and I intentionally avoided naming my employers directly. The association I worked for is an "association" of churches (technically called a "denomination"). The first church I served (which has since closed) was relatively small, while the second and third are larger congregations commonly referred to as "megachurches." Unlike the first two, the third church is independent and not affiliated with a denomination.

I'd also like to clarify something about the leader at the third church, who was considered "tough to work for." That reputation didn't stem from a lack of fairness or character. He is a strong leader with an excellent track record. In fact, during my brief time working with him, he treated me with respect and showed me kindness I didn't deserve.

AFTERWORD: OUCH!

1. Lawn Doctor (n.d.), *How to Scalp a Lawn: When Is the Best Time?*, accessed 21 April 2025, <https://www.lawndoctor.com/blog/do-you-need-scalp-your-lawn>.
2. Scripture quotations are taken from the New American Standard Bible, © 1971 by The Lockman Foundation.
3. Ibid., Philippians 1:6
4. Ibid., Matthew 16:26a
5. Ibid., John 10:10

RESOURCES

Be sure to download the E+R=O Resources and Programs mentioned throughout this book at:

KentJulian.com/ResponseBook

ABOUT THE AUTHOR

Kent Julian is many things—a family man, champion swim coach, business owner, CSP* professional speaker, fish taco lover, and proud bald guy. But it wasn't always this way. He began life as an at-risk child with severe learning challenges and SAT scores so low, he had to take Developmental Studies courses just to get into college—on probation.

From these humble beginnings, Kent went on to work with youth organizations and eventually became the Executive Director of a national youth association, driven to support teenagers facing similar challenges to those he experienced. Then, after 20 years in nonprofit work, he took a bold step and launched two successful businesses from scratch.

Along the way, Kent realized that his successes were never truly his own. Whether he was working with Millennials and Gen Z students, coaching championship swim teams, leading businesses, or speaking to organizations and associations, the positive results he experienced stemmed from the team members he was privileged to lead and the mentors who invested in his life.

Now, with expertise in leadership, corporate culture, and employee engagement, Kent is privileged to speak, write, and consult with leaders and teams across the country on what it takes to create an E+R=O culture.

Kent is also the author of multiple books, including *Who Wants To Be Normal, Anyway?!* and *How to Get Your Teen to Talk to You.*

To find out more, visit KentJulian.com.

> **CSP stands for Certified Speaking Professional with the National Speakers Association (NSA). It is the highest designation a speaker can earn with the NSA. Fewer than 800 professional speakers worldwide have earned this award, underscoring its rarity in the speaking business.*

INVITE KENT TO KEYNOTE YOUR NEXT EVENT!

Kent's goal as a speaker is to add so much value that he becomes your standard of excellence for the speakers you hire. He will be actively involved in your event from start to finish—before he arrives, when he's onstage, when he's offstage, and after the event wraps up.

Additionally, he customizes every presentation for your audience and prides himself on being the easiest speaker in the world to work with.

KentJulian.com/Speaking
booking@kentjulian.com
678-466-9482

JOURNAL

JOURNAL

JOURNAL

JOURNAL

JOURNAL

www.ingramcontent.com/pod-product-compliance
Lightning Source LLC
Chambersburg PA
CBHW032035290426
44110CB00012B/819